How We Argue

This accessible book provides a practical discussion of the main elements of argumentation as illustrated by 30 public arguments from a recent year on a wide variety of social, cultural, and scientific topics.

Arguing is an important form of communication in any society and a principal way in which ideas are exposed, discussed, and modified. The real-life examples examined in this book reflect the different considerations that go into composing arguments and the range of strategies that can be chosen as vehicles for our positions. They demonstrate the roles that emotion can play along with other modes of conveying evidence, from the use of images to the use of gestures. They show the power of threats, comparisons, and consequences. What emerges is an instructive discussion that illustrates the way we argue and that shows argument, invention, and evaluation in action.

This book is a stimulating read for anyone interested in argument and public discourse and can be used as a supplemental text for courses in argumentation, persuasive communication, critical thinking, composition, and informal logic.

Christopher W. Tindale is Director of the Centre for Research in Reasoning, Argumentation, and Rhetoric (CRRAR) and Distinguished University Professor at the University of Windsor, Canada.

How We Argue
30 Lessons in Persuasive Communication

Christopher W. Tindale

NEW YORK AND LONDON

First published 2023
by Routledge
605 Third Avenue, New York, NY 10158

and by Routledge
4 Park Square, Milton Park, Abingdon, Oxon, OX14 4RN

Routledge is an imprint of the Taylor & Francis Group, an informa business

© 2023 Christopher W. Tindale

The right of Christopher W. Tindale to be identified as author of this work has been asserted in accordance with sections 77 and 78 of the Copyright, Designs and Patents Act 1988.

All rights reserved. No part of this book may be reprinted or reproduced or utilised in any form or by any electronic, mechanical, or other means, now known or hereafter invented, including photocopying and recording, or in any information storage or retrieval system, without permission in writing from the publishers.

Trademark notice: Product or corporate names may be trademarks or registered trademarks, and are used only for identification and explanation without intent to infringe.

ISBN: 9781032353128 (hbk)
ISBN: 9781032353135 (pbk)
ISBN: 9781003326328 (ebk)

DOI: 10.4324/9781003326328

Typeset in Times New Roman
by codeMantra

Contents

List of figures ix
Acknowledgments xi

Introduction 1

PART I
The nature of argument 5

1 "Traditional" argument (the power of deduction) 7
2 Counterargument: the power of rebuttal (what can be trusted?) 11
3 Numbers matter (arguing with the use of polls) 15
4 Know your audience (rhetorical address) 19
5 Arguments and definitions (cults and presidents) 23
6 Saying less but meaning more (the use of hidden reasons) 27
7 Argument and explanation (what it all means) 32
8 Seeing is believing (the power of an image) 35
9 Moral argument (what is fair?) 39

PART II
Rhetorical argumentation 43

10 Arguing in silence (the power of a pause) 45

11 What's in a gesture? (racism in an act of dismissal) 49

12 Say it again (the power of repetition) 53

13 Argument and satire (what do we do with the children?) 58

14 Turning the tables (who would be worse?) 63

15 Emotional appeal (a call to aid) 67

PART III
Character-based argumentation 73

16 Praising character (the best amongst us) 75

17 Reflecting values (an excellent choice) 79

18 Bad behavior (a failure of character) 82

19 Damning character (the worse amongst us) 86

20 Associations (the company we keep) 90

21 The power of the expert (who you are and what you know matters) 95

PART IV
Strategies of reason 101

22 Using threats (let this be a warning) 103

23 Establishing precedents (what we do now matters later) 107

24 A causal chain (if this, then that) 111

25 Negative consequences (if this, then also that) 115

26 An unexpected outcome (the benefit of a pandemic)	119
27 For example (lessons from a case in point)	123
28 Argument and analogy (comparing cases)	127
29 A sign of the times (what do masks mean?)	132

PART V
Epilogue: how *we* argue — 137

30 A robot's point of view — 139

Sources — 143
Index — 153

Figures

8.1 Breonna Taylor, Louisville Billboards, August
     2020. Internet meme   35
28.1 1885 Anti-vaccination pamphlet (Archive of the
     National Library of Canada)   129

Acknowledgments

As I note in the Introduction, this short book has its origins in the Twitter feed "Argument of the Week," where a good corpus of arguments has accumulated over the years, each of which reflects a major event of the week. So, I am grateful to those who have been following the updates each week and making the occasional comment. I am particularly grateful to Michael Baumtrog, who supported the initiative at the outset in more ways than one, and who continues to encourage it on a weekly basis.

Some of these analyses have been shared with small audiences over the last year, mainly in classrooms and online discussions. As always, I am appreciative of the feedback received, some of which has led to corrections and improvements.

I am also grateful to Brian Eschrich, my editor at Routledge, for supporting the project, and to several anonymous reviewers for their constructive comments.

Introduction

The nature of arguments and the many different ways in which they appear can be as confusing as they are fascinating. Arguing (in the non-adversarial sense) is a primary form of communication in any society and a principal way in which ideas are exposed, discussed, and modified. It leads to consent and dissent. It perpetuates stereotypes and resolves injustices. It reinforces the status quo and moves social policies forward. It enlightens and disappoints, sparks the imagination, and reveals the darker side of human nature. Argument is, then, a powerful force. Neutral in nature, it can be turned to positive or negative ends. It always rewards serious investigation because it tells us something about ourselves, our fears and accomplishments, our strengths and our weaknesses. It mirrors us at our best, and sometimes at our worse.

In an academic paper now some decades old, American communication scholar Wayne Brockriede raised the question, "Where is Argument?" It may seem a strange question to pose, but it is one to which I'm particularly sensitive in preparing this short book. Note that Brockriede did not ask "what is an argument?" But his approach provides an interesting indirect response to that question as well. It turns out that, for him, arguments are found in people rather than in statements separated from the contexts in which they arise and operate. So, if we are interested in finding arguments, we should look at people. And given the great diversity we know exists among people, we might expect considerable diversity (although not as great) among arguments. For Brockriede, argument is potentially anywhere and everywhere because it is a human process. A process not just of communicating, but of perceiving things and then conveying that perception in the communication. We will return to some of Brockriede's ideas in the analyses ahead. My approach to arguments in this book is informed by his insights.

2 Introduction

In what follows, I explore the features and varieties of argument through discussion of 30 examples that were available on various media sources in 2020. The examples themselves stem from a simple Twitter project started in January of 2019: "Argument of the Week." Each week, I selected an argument from a source of interest and tweeted it. I began choosing arguments that interested me or that I thought were particularly bad. But over time, I came to select an argument that represented a major issue of that week, local, national, or international. I selected them irrespective of their strengths, and rarely made any judgment about their quality. By the end of the year, I had many of the major events that had occurred reflected in arguments.

This is a different kind of book, then, with brief focused discussions of different arguments. I took as my inspiration Brian Dillon's (2020) fascinating book, *Suppose a Sentence*, in which he builds short discussions around different sentences, often using a sentence to delve deeper into a writer's work. I have tried something similar with arguments, taking what has been used as an opportunity to explore a different dimension of how we argue, and the specific matters associated with different strategic choices. The Dutch author Cees Nooteboom (2021) writes a "book of days" to capture "the occasional something from the stream of what you think, what you read, what you see." What I see, read, and think about are arguments as they emerge from and reflect the social and political issues that concern us, and these are the occasional somethings that caught my attention. There are examples that reflect international and national concerns, and at the end of the book sources are provided for each argument. I encourage you to explore these sources, to do the research, to discover more about the arguers involved and their circumstances.

The examples I discuss here are all sourced from events in 2020. Little justification is needed to explain why this particular year was chosen. It was the year of COVID-19, of lockdowns and panic, anti-expert rhetoric and health authorities struggling to master the ins and outs of effective communication. But it was also the year of social unrest most vividly seen in the Black Lives Matter movement, as well as the year of a presidential campaign in the United States unlike any seen before, if only for its contested results.

Occasionally, the examples I chose to tweet elicited a strong response from people who were encouraged or incensed by the sentiments of an argument. But I also, occasionally, received the question "Is this an argument?" In the following, I find the space to make a reply.

There are some important distinctions in the study of argument that influence the choice of which discourses to include. Traditionally, the arguments that have been the subject of academic study have tended to involve a focus on what are called formal relations between the parts. Where evidence is provided for a claim, the statements conveying that evidence are called premises, and the claim is called the conclusion. In strong arguments, the conclusion follows from the premises and the arguments are judged to be valid. Beyond "following from," a second principal criterion of strength is that the premises be acceptable or true. A valid argument with acceptable premises was judged to be sound. So, two primary questions came to the fore: is the inference on which the argument depends valid? And is the argument sound?

This traditional approach has serious limitations, and people who study arguments have insisted that we need to expand our understanding beyond the focus on formal relationships, particularly if we are going to appreciate how arguments arise in the everyday contexts in which we encounter them. This is not to deny that some arguments do meet the conditions of formal strength; it's just that there are many more arguments that do not and yet still have merit. More importantly, this larger non-formal class of arguments is what we are more likely to encounter in our daily exchanges. So, among the arguments that are discussed in this collection, there will be very few of the so-called traditional variety, and many more that challenge our appreciation of what should count as good (or bad) reasoning and why.

In recent decades, the interest in understanding arguments has shifted, both in and outside the classroom, to include a study of what is called informal logic. The title "informal" is perhaps not the best, but it indicates a contrast to what was taken to be formal. Informal logicians are interested in capturing arguments "in the wild," and so draw from the wealth of contexts that people like Wayne Brockriede identified (while not including Brockriede amongst their ranks). This gives rise to an advantage and a disadvantage. The arguments discussed and assessed are immediately more recognizable as the kinds of arguments we might see or hear or use as we go about our lives. They are not divorced from the dynamic situations in which they arose. But this very animation makes them more slippery and difficult to capture in careful appreciations. They emerge from contexts that include other types of discourse, and so the material of interest (including the relevant participants) needs to be identified and extracted. The criteria that informal logicians use to evaluate arguments extend far beyond the interests in formal validity and soundness to include considerations of what is acceptable (and to whom), what is relevant (a variety of the traditional measure of "following from"), and whether there is enough support for a conclusion.

Another American theorist, Daniel O'Keefe, helped separate the considerations I have been discussing in a distinction between what he called argument^1 and argument^2, taking the examination beyond the simple formal/informal contrast. For O'Keefe, when people are involved in the process of arguing with each other they are involved in argument^2; when one of them makes an argument—as a product—they produce an argument^1. Of course, cases of argument^2 will include one or more argument^1. But it is argument^2 that captures the kinds of exchanges that characterize many situations in which argument occurs. In the following collection, we will find examples where argument^1 is embedded within an argument^2.

All this serves as a way to prepare you for the rich variety of arguments that are ahead, sometimes arising in surprising packages. We will find Donald Trump conveying arguments via the medium of Twitter that necessitates short, abbreviated thoughts—a format that suits the rhetorical force of his contributions. And Joe Biden turning an opponent's charge back upon that opponent. Arguments conveyed through gesture, image, and satire. Arguments interwoven with explanations and emotional reactions. Arguments in the form of threats, predictions, and powerful silences. Arguments that appeal to the qualities of a person's character; and arguments that criticize the deficiencies of a person's character.

Where, then, is argument? Wherever we gather to explore issues and the responses made to those issues. And one further question: When is argument? When circumstances arise that challenge, threaten, and demand a response. Circumstances, often of our own making, that question the common ground that underlies a society. The year 2020 was rife with such circumstances.

Part I
The nature of argument

1 "Traditional" argument (the power of deduction)

Argument #1

> Today we are asked whether the land these treaties promised remains an Indian reservation for purposes of federal criminal law. Because Congress has not said otherwise, we hold the government to its word.
>
> US Justice Gorsuch

In July 2020, the US Supreme Court passed down a ruling that found about half of Oklahoma to be Native American land. Justice Neil Gorsuch wrote the majority opinion, from which our example derives. The reasoning here exhibits features that may be more familiar to people when they think about arguments. Many of us learned in some formal setting that arguments are, well, formal. That is, they fit regular patterns which can be "translated" into symbols to show the validity of the reasoning. The standard here is called "deductive." That is, given the premises, we can deduce a conclusion that has to follow. There is an element of compulsion involved. If we want to be reasonable, we are committed to a conclusion given the premises that are provided for it (here, "premises" is a technical name for the reasons given in support of a claim).

Justice Gorsuch indicates this kind of compulsion in his judgment. The thinking here is that the US government had promised the land in a legal treaty (a premise); Congress (the agency of the government) has not said otherwise (another premise). It follows from this that the land still belongs to those to whom it was promised. There's no wriggle room here; it's more than saying a promise is a promise. A legally binding obligation exists until it is superseded. In fact, the judgment suggests the land would belong to the tribes involved in perpetuity.

DOI: 10.4324/9781003326328-3

The case before the court (*McGirt v. Oklahoma*) arose after, McGirt, a member of the Seminole Nation of Oklahoma had been convicted of sex crimes on Creek land. He later argued that the state lacked jurisdiction in the case, and he should be retried in a federal court. In agreeing, the high court noted that, for the purposes of the Major Crimes Act, "land reserved for the Creek Nation since the 19th-century remains 'Indian country'." While the dissenting opinion from four Justices stressed the judgment would create havoc with respect to past convictions that could now be revisited, and while some commentators saw the judgment as a result of close textual reading, for our purposes it is simply a matter of good logical inference.

For a long time, arguments where the premises (if true) guaranteed the conclusion were simply called deductive arguments. Now, people who study these things prefer to refer to a standard of strength rather than a type of argument. Other standards involve induction and plausibility. We will see these operating in some later examples.

And also for a long time, "argument" itself was treated as almost synonymous with arguments that possessed this deductive standard. This was very much *the* argument of the standard logic course experienced by generations of students. Starting around the middle of the last century, this thinking began to be seriously challenged. These formal arguments had their place, but they couldn't accommodate the rich variety of ways in which arguments are important in our lives. The many different types of argument that we will explore through the examples of this book illustrate this point.

As much as these are traditional arguments, some contemporary theorists question whether this kind of reasoning should count as arguing at all. If the outcome is self-evident, for example, then according to Belgian theorist Chaim Perelman, what we have is demonstration rather than argumentation. No one needs to argue about what is self-evident, he insisted. On his terms, "argument" should be reserved for reasoning about conclusions that are uncertain. Similarly, Wayne Brockriede looked for what he called an "inferential leap" from beliefs that are already held to a new belief that the arguer wants us to hold. In reasoning that is characterized by the deductive standard, where the premises entail the conclusion (that is, it follows necessarily from them), then there is no inferential leap. So, for Brockriede, there is no argument.

I have included an example of "formal argument" because, as I noted above, most readers will be familiar with it. Those of us who learned logic in the classroom were fed on examples like: "Socrates is human, and all human beings are mortal. Therefore, Socrates is mortal." This is a classic example of a valid Aristotelian syllogism. It is called a syllogism, a technical term, because it involves a collection of propositions from which one follows necessarily after the others have been stated—a proof. It is called Aristotelian after the Ancient Greek thinker Aristotle who devised a system of syllogistic reasoning that served as the standard of argument for centuries. And it is called "valid" because that is the term of correctness used when a conclusion is entailed in this way by the premises (otherwise, it is invalid).

While Perelman and Brockriede have a point, this reasoning can still play an important role in everyday argumentation, even if it is only a limited one. Some psychologists believe the human mind often makes use of a deductive principle in "seeing" what follows, and advertisers can exploit this. When we hear an advertising jingle like "the bigger the burger the better the burger; the burgers are better at Burger King" most of us have no difficulty completing the reasoning and inferring that the burgers must be better at Burger King. In fact, whoever wrote the jingle was relying on our ability to do that; otherwise the costs of a huge advertising campaign may all be for nothing. Of course, most people will also see that while the conclusion we draw follows from the premises and was intended to do so, the weak link in the reasoning is the premise that "the bigger the burger the better the burger." In deciding the quality of burgers, size may not be a factor. It is a disputable premise, and if someone were to offer evidence for *it*, *then* Brockriede and Perelman would say we were in an area where an argument is likely to show up.

In the case of the Supreme Court argument under consideration, the statements need to be adjusted and interpreted in light of the full judgment (a link to the judgment is available under "Sources") to see the flow of the reasoning.

Premise 1: Congress promised these lands as a reservation for the Creek Nation in the treaty of 1833. [The 1833 Treaty fixed borders for a "permanent home to the whole Creek Nation of Indians" for "so long as they shall exist as a nation, and continue to occupy the country hereby assigned to them."]
Premise 2: Once a federal reservation is established, only Congress can diminish or disestablish it. Doing so requires a clear expression of congressional intent.

Premise 3: Congress has not said otherwise, we hold the government to its word.

Conclusion: The land these treaties promised remains an Indian reservation for purposes of federal criminal law.

The three premises work together to guarantee the conclusion. That is, if they are all correct and acceptable, the conclusion follows from them. We would be caught in a contradiction were we to admit the premises as a set but deny the conclusion. Congress established the reservation; only Congress can disestablish it; Congress has not disestablished it. Therefore, the land in question remains an Indian reservation. That the "land in question" constitutes about half of the state of Oklahoma is what caught people's attention and led to the headlines. As the Dean of the Law School at the University of Iowa, a citizen of the Chickasaw Nation of Oklahoma, noted, "Now and then there's a great case that helps you keep the faith about the rule of law, and this is one of those."

2 Counterargument
The power of rebuttal (what can be trusted?)

Argument #2

> If anything [mail-in voting] tends to favor Republicans because the people ... who historically have tended to vote most often by mail are elderly people, people over 65, and they tend to vote more Republican than Democratic.
> Chris Wallace, Interviewed on Fox News, May 25, 2020

When confronted with an argument, there are various ways to respond. We might agree with the position completely, or agree in part but argue it's not such a bad thing; or one might offer alternative outcomes to show that the original argument was too restricted in its scope—but nothing works as well as a counterargument if it's well developed. A strong counterargument in the form of a rebuttal or refutation eliminates the original claim and clears the ground for fresh reflection.

There is a storied tradition of such reasoning strategies in Western philosophical thought, starting with the Socratic method, something that will be familiar to many readers. In many examples provided by Plato, Socrates would enter into a discussion with an expert in order to discover the nature of some important concept, like courage or justice. The expert would provide a definition of the concept and Socrates would proceed to develop a refutation argument by showing that the expert's definition (A) led, through a series of logical steps, to a contradiction (not-A). According to accounts, this type of argument was a favored way of teaching students in Plato's Academy.

Not all counterarguments are so strong, and rebuttals (rather than refutations) may simply give good reasons to show that another position or argument is just wrong. Or, as theorist Stephen Toulmin pointed out, rebuttals can show an exception to a conclusion. As he phrased matters, a conclusion would follow from a set of data and a supporting warrant "unless" there was an exception that defeated or rebutted the conclusion. In the case we are considering here, a highly contentious issue had arisen in the 2020 US federal election concerning the reliability of mail-in ballots. As was widely reported, President Trump claimed a number of times that mail-in ballots were problematic and susceptible to fraud. In support of the president's position, the National Republican Congressional Committee argued that the push for increased mail-in ballots was an attempt by democrats to rig the election and steal it from Trump. This was the point that Washington journalist Chris Wallace focused on in pushing back against the claim. At the time, Wallace was a broadcast journalist with Fox News Channel.

In the specific argument we are considering, Wallace isn't arguing against the claim that mail-in ballots are susceptible to large-scale fraud. He does make this claim in the interview, saying that he has done some "deep diving" on the issue (which we can assume is a reference to careful research) and has found no record of mass fraud, although there have been instances of it (favoring both parties, it seems). His point in the argument, though, is that increased mail-in ballots would more likely favor the republicans, and so would not lead to democrats stealing the election. Essentially, on his argument, the republicans and Trump should have nothing to fear from increased mail-in ballots.

The results of his investigation, then, show that "If anything, [mail-in voting] tends to favor republicans." This is because (for the reason that) the people most likely to use mail-in ballots in the past have been elderly people over 65, and that demographic is more likely to vote republican than democrat. So, he has two premises or reasons linked together (that is, they depend on each other to support the conclusion) for the conclusion that mail-in voting is more likely to favor republicans. This is a clear counterargument to the claim that mail-in ballots would favor the democrats (which was the position espoused by the National Republican Congressional Committee). Wallace is saying that, even if Trump is right about mail-in ballots (although he believes he is not), that's not a bad thing for him. Is he right?

To consider the merits of Wallace's argument, we need to do two things: we need to ask whether his claim is supported by the reasons he provides, that is, does it follow from them? Then, we need to review both of his premises independently, although if one is weak, it will weaken the other since they work in combination.

If we are satisfied with the argument on both of these criteria, we ask whether it is a good counterargument to the republican position.

The conclusion is that mail-in voting tends to favor republicans. We can look at that claim and asks ourselves "what sort of evidence would we expect in support of it?" That is, why would someone believe such a claim? Well, we would expect to be told something about the nature of mail-in voters. Who, historically, has used this system? We would also want to know what ties such a group to republicans. Wallace's premises meet both of these expectations. So, we can say, they provide the right kind of evidence.

Then we move to the premises themselves. Are they acceptable? The first premise reads "people most likely to use mail-in ballots in the past have been elderly people over 65." We don't know if this is correct, but it is the kind of factual claim that can be verified. The statistics exist that would tell us the degree to which Wallace is right. Given that he claims to have dived deep in researching the issue, we can give him the benefit of the doubt. But the important thing is that it is verifiable (unlike a claim like, say, "people tend not to like going out to vote when the weather is too cold"). The second premise reads, "elderly people over 65 are more likely to vote republican than democrat." This is a very similar claim to the first premise in that it also reports the kind of statistical data that would be accessible. It would help the case if Wallace had said something about his sources, and perhaps the onus was on the person interviewing him to ask for this. But, again, this can come down to a matter of trust. As a Washington journalist, his professional reputation depends to some degree on his trustworthiness in what he reports. So, we can accept his evidence in principle, with the understanding that if necessary it can be verified.

As a counterargument, the above judgment must be stacked up against the argument to which it is responding. The Fox News report in which the Wallace interview is embedded includes several relevant remarks. President Trump attacked mail-in ballots, insisting on the likelihood of fraud "without citing specific evidence." And

> Most recently, Republican National Committee, National Republican Congressional Committee and California Republican Party sued Gov. Gavin Newsom and the state's Secretary of State Alex Padilla on Sunday, claiming an executive order sending mail-in ballots to all registered voters in the state is an "illegal power grab" that invites potential fraud.

In the course of this lawsuit, the claim of potential (or previous widespread) fraud was not supported by any evidence. As it transpired, the case was voluntarily withdrawn on the 9th of July after the California Assembly passed a law to achieve the same result as Newsome had tried to achieve.

So, we have on one side evidence that is in principle verifiable and which one source claims to have verified through research. We have no reasons to doubt the truthfulness of that source. On the other hand, the charges of massive fraud, although repeated in several contexts, were never verified (and other media sources have claimed independently that the evidence does not exist). So, on balance, Wallace's argument seems the stronger of the two. The counterargument is effective.

That has been the point here, to show something of the nature of counter-argumentation and to consider when and why it can be successful. In principle, all arguments are open to the possibility of rebuttal or refutation—of counter-argumentation. That is the nature of the activity we are exploring here, as it arises in the everyday contexts of social exchanges. No argument is immune to objection, and we should always be skeptical when claims are made that suggest one is. At the end of the day, it is how those objections are expressed and whether the original argument can withstand them that matters.

3 Numbers matter (arguing with the use of polls)

Argument #3

> If the election were held today, Mr. Biden would win the presidency, even if the polls were exactly as wrong as four years ago. The reason is simple: His lead is far wider than Hillary Clinton's was in the final polls and large enough to withstand another 2016 meltdown.
>
> Nate Cohn, *New York Times*, July 16, 2020

This argument, asserted in the *New York Times*, draws its reasoning from the art of polling. This is a common way of deriving information about large groups of people and what they think. An appropriate selection of people is canvassed for their opinions, the group canvassed is taken to be representative of a general population, and so a general conclusion is drawn about such a population. While the standard of measure in Argument #1 was deductive, the standard here is what is called "inductive." A general conclusion is drawn on the basis of a sample of evidence. How strong the argument is will depend in part on how strong the sample is. There are no guarantees about the conclusion here—as we have seen with some polls that got things spectacularly wrong, a phenomenon to which this argument actually refers. In 2016, most polls showed Hillary Clinton to have a considerable lead over Donald Trump. They were wrong. How could this happen?

In fact, just the next month of 2020 (August 29), filmmaker and activist Michael Moore warned people to expect the same result as happened in 2016:

> when CNN polled registered voters in August in just the swing states, Biden and Trump were in a virtual tie. In Minnesota, it's 47-47. In Michigan, where Biden had a big lead, Trump has closed the gap to 4 points. Are you ready for a Trump victory?

We do need to be very careful when reading arguments that are drawn from polls, because often those arguments depend on interpretations of the data that has been amassed. In the first instance, it matters how the sample of people who have been questioned were chosen. The argument from the *New York Times* claims Biden would win the election (if it were held July 19) even if the polls were as wrong as in 2016. The evidence supporting this is that he has a much wider lead than Clinton had, sufficient to withstand a "meltdown." For this conclusion to hold, the evidence of a strong Biden lead must be drawn from polling samples that represent all dimensions of eligible voters in the United States. We need to look at the polling evidence behind the stated premise: "His lead is far wider than Hillary Clinton's was in the final polls."

The article from which the argument is extracted provides the information we need to assess the reasoning. Correspondent Nate Cohn collates the polling results for the highly contested "battleground states"[1] in two columns: one gives the straightforward results, assuming they are reliable. This column has Biden winning 390 electoral colleges, showing leads in all of the crucial states. The second column adjusts the results to assume the polls are off as much as they were in 2016. Here, Biden wins 310 electoral colleges, still considerably more than the 270 a candidate needs to become president. This column shows Biden ahead of Trump in all but North Carolina. The 2020 poll averages were based on surveys that had been conducted since June 1 by FiveThirtyEight, an American website that focuses on, among other things, opinion poll analyses. This company collates the results of polls from established companies like Ipsos and Pulse Opinion Research.

As I mentioned, the key thing in deciding whether this information can be trusted is determining whether the samples on which the results are based were representative. Ideally, we look for randomly selected samples, where any member of a demographic has a chance of being chosen. Too many polls involve answers from people who "opt-in," or via media (like websites) to which only selective populations have access. In either case, the samples are not randomly selected.

Cohn is aware of this issue and looks closely at how the poll results were obtained, because the crux of what motivates his study is whether polls can be trusted after 2016 (when they predicted a strong win for Clinton). The key factor that he identifies changing since 2016 is that "many pollsters now weight their sample to properly represent voters without a college degree." Not doing this in

2016 is widely believed to be one of the reasons that the support for Trump was underestimated. But it was only one of the reasons, and education was not sufficient to account for the size of the error. Other factors were in play, like turnout. Pollsters, influenced by the response to Obama, for example, overestimated the likely turnout among the Black population.

One of the most popular ways by which pollsters collect information is through telephone surveys, and people who agree to speak to surveyors "are likelier to be volunteers. They are likelier to express trust in their neighbors and society." Now, the first thing we might ask here is how Mr. Cohn and others know what people are likelier to do or believe? And I suspect you've guessed the answer. This "knowledge" is drawn from other surveys. So, polling results support the trust we have in the science of polling (and on the other side, we have the widely reported cases where the polling is spectacularly wrong—as in 2016). But more importantly, if reliable, this information tells us that one means of collecting data—through telephone surveys—may be biased. Another means of deriving information is through panel surveys, where people agree to be contacted periodically to have their opinions (and changes of opinion) measured. Again, we can see that this is not random.

So, as much as the science of polling may have been adjusted between 2016 and 2020, there are still serious issues that may undermine the reliability of results. That is why in his argument Cohn makes the effort to emphasize that even if the polls are off, Biden is still far enough ahead for this to not make a difference.

Ultimately, we are not given the information we need to really judge the argument we have. We don't know about the various polls, how they were conducted, what questions were asked and of whom. Were states proportionately represented in samples (that is, more from larger states, fewer from smaller states)? And were those samples representative of other differences beyond education, like race, gender, and age? We don't know these things really because that's not the kind of article Cohn is writing. We would need to dig deeper into the research he depends on by looking at the polls collated by FiveThirtyEight and how *they* were conducted. That would be a lot of work, and so we depend on analyses like the one here. But my point is that, as an argument, it draws attention to the importance of polling as a way to draw generalized, reliable conclusions about large populations of people. And we have considered how to test the reliability of those conclusions, even though such tests will often demand considerable work on our part as we sort through the studies that have been done and look at how they have been done.

Polling gives information for strong arguments, but not ones that guarantee their conclusion. That's because, as we've seen, all kinds of variables can creep in to shift the outcomes. And, as Cohn notes, there were still four months to go before the election and people's opinions could change. After all, the four years of Trump's presidency and the period leading up to it saw a decline of trust in experts and the media and things like polling!

For such reasons, polling companies will continue to refine their procedures so that those who rely on them for information will not lose faith in them. Four months after the piece in *The New York Times*, Biden beat Trump by 306 to 232 electoral colleges. We know the fallout that resulted from that election and the controversy that surrounded those numbers. But they did prove the numbers in Cohn's second column close to right. That was the column that allowed the polls could be off as much as they were in 2016; that was the column that gave Biden 310. So, time proved the argument correct, Biden wins the presidency even if the polls were as wrong as four years before. Not very reassuring for our trust in polling arguments. Or maybe the result was just coincidence.

Note

1 Arizona, Florida, Michigan, North Carolina, Wisconsin.

4 Know your audience (rhetorical address)

Argument #4

> The fact that the virus is no respecter of individuals, whoever they are, is one of the reasons why we do need to have strict social distancing measures so that we can reduce the rate of infection.
>
> Michael Gove, March 27, 2020

Reported by the BBC, the speaker here is Michael Gove, a Cabinet Office minister in Boris Johnson's UK government, and it follows the diagnosis of Johnson in March 2020 with COVID-19. The argument illustrates a case of using an example to make a general point. But, of course, Gove is saying more than this, because it is the *who* of the example that supposedly carries weight here. He is responding to a questioner who asked whether the prime minister should have been "better protected," and while his response is not a direct answer, it is relevant none the less. The thinking behind Gove's argument is that the virus is no respecter of status; if it can infect the prime minister, it can infect anyone. Coming at a period of the pandemic when people still needed to be persuaded of the dangers involved and the need to take specific cautions, then this argument adds to a general set of advocacy arguments that were being communicated during the early months of 2020.

Advocacy arguments have a variety of related goals, but chief among this is a desire to bring about an action or behavior in a specific audience, based on a change of belief. Here, Gove is specifically advocating for social distancing as a specific behavior that would lead to a reduction in the rate of infection (the ultimate goal). And the evidence used to advocate for this is the case of Johnson's diagnosis. How compelling is this example for Gove's purpose? To answer that we should consider the *audience* that Gove is addressing.

DOI: 10.4324/9781003326328-6

The rhetorical tradition has a history of instructing arguers to "know the audience," and indeed, audience is a crucial factor in considering the power and even the composition of arguments. Because what argument a speaker or writer chooses to employ should depend on the audience to be addressed—what is its makeup, what beliefs does it hold, and how open or hostile is it likely to be to the message being argued? A failure to understand the audience for which an argument is intended is one of the likely reasons for a failure of persuasion.

Aristotle identified three kinds of audience that he judged were important. The first, relevant to legal considerations, was a forensic audience—one that judged the past and came to some decision about it. A second, relevant to political concerns, is a deliberative audience—one who judges the future about what ought to be done, how to act. Both of these audiences, we see, are judges. The third and last audience is identified as a spectator audience, and the arguments in question are ceremonial. On such occasions, speakers have the opportunity to stress the values of a society, reinforcing what it is that makes us the strong community that we are. Some values are promoted, and other behaviors (deemed blameworthy) are to be avoided. We will see this vividly illustrated in some of the later examples.

While these three audiences are given separate analyses, it should be clear (as it was for Aristotle) that any particular argument could combine features of more than one, with several types of audience in mind. We can see that with Gove's argument. It is first and foremost aimed at a deliberative audience, but there are elements of the other two. We see the virus is no respecter of status because of who, in the past and now, has been infected. And the need to adopt measures that will reduce the rate of infection implicitly promotes a value of care and concern for others.

Arguments should, minimally, begin where an audience "lives," take up residence in ideas that are familiar to them, drawing attention to beliefs they already hold. Then, through various strategies, the audience can be led from that recognized and comfortable ground to a position that, while new, appears plausible in light of the common base from which the reasoning began and the choice of the strategy by which the argument is conveyed.

Of course, it will be easier to accomplish this with an audience that is open to the message, or previously predisposed to accept it because it reinforces a position already widely held. The hardest audience to address is the one that is hostile. That is, the message conveyed in the argument challenges (maybe directly opposes) a position on which this audience relies. Finding common ground with a hostile audience puts an arguer's skills of invention to the most severe test.

Most politicians think carefully about what they say, and so we might expect an element of design in Gove's argument. He is not, that is, speaking off the cuff. His audience, addressed through the intermediary of the press, is the British public, a composite audience made up of all three factors just discussed—the open, the persuaded, and the hostile. Each will receive the example of Johnson's infection in a slightly different way, but each is also likely to process this evidence in a way consistent with what Gove might have hoped.

Those already predisposed to the need for social distancing will see this as further confirmation for the position they already hold. They, in turn, might repeat the argument to friends who may be skeptics. The Johnson diagnosis thereby becomes a warning meme replicating through society. Those who had yet to be convinced either way, but who were open to evidence for and against social distancing, should judge this relevant to their concerns. The burden of proof, should they recognize it as such, lies with them to accept the reason into their deliberations unless they can counter it in some clear way (which is to say that the burden of proof does not lie with Gove to defend his point further).

The hostile audience must also consider how they could rebut such an argument. Gove is not basing his position on a judgment that might be questioned or an interpretation that could be challenged. That is, his evidence is not subjective. He is appealing to a fact about the world—Johnson's verified diagnosis. In spite of what is often claimed, facts do not "speak for themselves"; they only mean what people explain them to mean. They are harder to dismiss or challenge than judgments. If skeptics believe there is a vague line dividing more "privileged" members of society from everyone else, then Johnson's example counters that skepticism, and this is what Gove is pressing. It is more difficult to argue unfairness in the prohibitions then being placed on certain activities, which may have made it seem that some segments of society were more disadvantaged than others. Gove is pointing to a strong equalizing factor. Laws may impact people in different ways. But the emergency that necessitates those laws does not discriminate.

On balance, Gove's is a good argument. Rooted in a state of affairs that is difficult to contest (unless it is believed that the whole Johnson diagnosis and subsequent hospitalization was a hoax—a tangent it is not worth exploring here), he gives a relevant reason for strict social distancing measures. And, of course, he also makes clear that this is just one reason for the claim he is making. In the contexts that the pandemic created in 2020, we are aware that there were others. Perhaps Gove could have strengthened his case by mentioning others. But in the short, "sound-bite" opportunity of an official statement, where details can often obscure the forest, he focuses on the key, pertinent factor that events of the day make available. No other reasons were needed; the example fully supported his case.

5 Arguments and definitions (cults and presidents)

Argument #5

> To see Trumpism as a cult is not to refuse to engage with its effects, the crimes committed in its name or the way it has awakened and emboldened the cruelest and most destructive beliefs and practices in the American playbook. Instead, the cult framework should relieve the pressure many of us feel to call Trumpites back to themselves, to keep arguing with them. They are stuck in a bad relationship with a controlling figure.
>
> Virginia Heffernan, January 10, 2020

Students of history can be forgiven for thinking the year is wrong on the above argument. But, no, Virginia Heffernan's piece appeared in the *Los Angeles Times* a year before President Trump's supporters stormed the US Capitol on January 6, 2021. It simply sets out a thesis that seems reinforced by that subsequent event. But the implications of this argument suggest the indications of what could occur were present long before the 2021 riot.

In this piece, journalist Heffernan approaches the Trump phenomenon not by asking about the figure at the center, but by exploring "the worshipful attitude so many Americans have toward him." And by employing the term "worshipful" early in her article, she announces the nature of the study she conducts, because her strategy in the piece is to assign Trumpism, as she calls it, to the category of a cult. This is clearly captured in the title of the article: "Call Trumpism what it is: A Cult."

Later in this book, we will explore examples of what is called analogical reasoning, but some readers may already recognize it at work in this example because in arguing that Trumpism is a cult, she needs to show similarities involved that fit the essential characteristics of a cult. But this is a specific kind of analogical reasoning

DOI: 10.4324/9781003326328-7

because it involves a *definition*. So, the strategy involved is to argue that a new phenomenon fits the classification of an established concept and by virtue of the fit it should be judged or treated as a member of that class. The new phenomenon is Trumpism, and the established concept or class is "being a cult."

Reasoning to and from definitions is an important way in which we use argument. Danish scholars Christian Kock and Lisa Villadsen, for example, use argument to arrive at a definition of "populism" in 2022 (a concept relevant to the domain of the current example). They suggest that populism is "claiming to speak on behalf of the people," a minimal definition, as they admit. In the context of political events leading up to 2020 and developing throughout the year, Heffernan might have approached her argument by using such a concept of "populism." But the fact that scholars are still arguing in 2022 for how it should be understood suggests it is a contested concept. Whereas the definition of "cult" is more established. So, unlike Kock and Villadsen who reason *to* a definition, Heffernan reasons *from* one. She takes a concept that already has wide acceptance and argues that the phenomenon surrounding Trump fits the description. In fact, she is using a particular pattern of reasoning. Also later in the text, we will explore such patterns of reasoning, identifying them as argumentation schemes. Heffernan's argument gives us an advance look at such a pattern:

- Premise: It is by virtue of having features a, b, c that something is classified as C.
- Premise: The primary subject has features a, b, c.
- Conclusion: The primary subject ought to be classified as C.

The letters in italics represent variables and any particular example of this argument scheme will have real features to replace those letters. And, we are not required to find three features or limited to that number. But, of course, we would expect that the more relevant similarities that are shared, the stronger the argument. In the second premise, I have referred to the "primary subject." In analogical arguments, that's the analogue or item about which a conclusion is drawn. So, it's appropriate to use that identifying term here.

You will recognize that the short argument at the head of the previous page doesn't fit this pattern in any straightforward way. That's because it is only a part of the Argument from Classification that Virginia Heffernan develops over the course of her article. She looks at recognized cults and claims about them in order to identify

Arguments and definitions (cults and presidents) 25

what she takes to be essential features of any cult (features that I call a, b, c). That comprehensive work takes up a lot of space, so it is not possible to collapse it into a simple version of the argument pattern. But all that work provides the context that will be explored when the argument is evaluated.

For example, Ms. Heffernan appeals to the authority of an expert on cults (and former Moonie) Steven Hassan for details of what makes up a cult, and she cites several other people, including religious leaders, who have used the term "cult" for Trump and his followers. From these and other sources, she extracts what appear to be features characteristic of cult members as follows:

i Republicans, according to polls, had "abandoned their commitment to libertarianism, family values or simple logic";
ii These same people are "lost to paranoia and factually unmoored talking points";
iii True believers undergo a "radical personal change" and become a different person;
iv The cult framework shows people "stuck in a bad relationship with a controlling figure."

From these features we can certainly get our variables for the first premise, four of them. If these same variables are also characteristic of Trumpism, then the conclusion has strong support.

What should we ask about any instance of this pattern that then gives us the criteria for exploring this particular example? Well, we want to be reassured that the identified features are characteristic of a cult and its members, and that they are essential (not incidental) features. And, crucially, we need to be clear that these features are characteristics of Trumpism, and also that there are no dissimilarities that would remove Trumpism from the classification.

The first point is reasonably well addressed in the article. As I have noted, there are appeals to relevant experts like Hassan and other sources that support the features identified, and it is reasonable on the basis of what is described there (and other research we might conduct into the nature of cults) to attribute these features to cults and see them, or at least (iii) and (iv), as essential characteristics of the concept involved.

Extending those features to Trump's followers is another matter, and one that it is understandably more difficult to support. Ms. Heffernan is aware of this. She makes reference to the statements made by evangelicals that seem to support the attribution, and she refers to other journalists who have related stories of people within the Trump camp who possess the characteristics she describes. But ultimately, she seems to allow that this falls a little short when she says: "What the cult diagnosis may lack in scholarly rigor, it makes up for in explanatory power." And at the end of the day, it is an explanation that people are after. Classifying the phenomenon as a cult provides a plausible explanation, one that would probably weigh against any dissimilarities that might be brought forward.

The sample argument we have from the larger analysis explains why it might be so difficult to argue with those she calls Trumpites. They are involved in a bad relationship with a controlling figure. On the basis of the classification argument she has provided, this explanation is given plausible support. What we mean by a term often illuminates how it should be understood in the contexts in which we find it operating. Virginia Heffernan's classificatory argument had great explanatory power in 2020 and, unfortunately, it still held a year later.

6 Saying less but meaning more (the use of hidden reasons)

Argument #6

> If health workers work without PPE (personal protective equipment) they are risking their lives, and that also risks the lives of the people they serve. It is criminal and it is a murder. And it has to stop.
>
> Dr. Tedros Ghebreyesus, August 21, 2020

The events of 2020 expanded our vocabulary in unexpected ways. One of those was a fast understanding of what was meant by "personal protective equipment" (PPE). Dr. Tedros Adhanom Ghebreyesus, Director General of the World Health Organization, is speaking here against what he describes as corruption related to PPE. He was responding to a journalist's comment about health professionals in some nations going on strike because they lack appropriate PPE, supposedly due to government corruption related to COVID-19 funds. In his full response, Tedros calls any level or type of corruption unacceptable, but that related to PPE is "actually murder."

Our question with respect to this argument is how he gets from an activity that risks the lives of health care workers and those they serve to a claim of "murder." There's a gap here that is characteristic of a lot of arguments. Especially on platforms where speakers or writers are constrained in how much they can say, compression is essential. But while a message may be compressed, those receiving it need to be able to reconstruct it in its entirety. They need to identify what is hidden and make it present. This is particularly important when we review arguments, because we need to be able to judge whether what is assumed in these gaps is acceptable. Sometimes, an arguer will leave unstated what is thought to be obvious. There's no point in saying it; everyone knows or accepts it. And, there can be

DOI: 10.4324/9781003326328-8

an advantage to leaving part of an argument unexpressed. Aristotle drew attention to this a long time ago. If arguers know their audiences well, they know what they can assume those audiences know and so they do not need to state those things. This requires that the audience then be able to supply what has been unstated, shifting them from a passive to an active role. Completing an argument in this way can make people more receptive of reasoning that they have "seen" for themselves.

There are also risks, of course, if the hidden element is not obvious and difficult to supply, then the audience may miss the point altogether, in which case the argument will likely fail to achieve any uptake. That's where the type of hidden component involved becomes important. Generally, these fall into two camps. First, there are the assumptions that people make whenever they communicate. If you think about it, we never say everything when we speak or write. We always depend upon a mass of shared understandings about the way the world works, the ways we behave, what language means, and so on. None of these things will be controversial. If we didn't make such assumptions and tried to cover everything, then our communications would be much longer and quite boring. An Anglo-American philosopher who studied conversation, Paul Grice, argued that successful communication depends on cooperation and that this involves following certain maxims (a maxim is a basic principle behind something). One of these, called a maxim of quantity, says "Make your contribution as informative as is required (for the current purpose of the exchange)." Obviously, this will depend upon the context involved, because in some we need to provide more information than in others. But the general advice behind the maxim is to think about what the context (and audience) requires and measure what you say accordingly: saying enough, but not too much (Grice was concerned that repetition or unnecessary information was confusing).

So, an unspoken element in an argument that involved a necessary assumption might be added in a reconstruction to show how a reason is relevant to a claim it seems intended to support. For example, someone who says, "we should meet our climate commitments because the future of our children depends on it," is assuming that future children will need a stable environment in which to flourish. That's not particularly controversial and is something with which most people will agree. It also provides the right kind of connection between the idea in the claim (meeting climate commitments) and that in the reason (children's future). Supplying it readily completes the argument. And some contexts would benefit from having it stated. Of course, we might choose to frame it in different ways. But, generally, we "see" the connection. The test we should make whenever we supply such a hidden assumption is to ask ourselves whether it's fair to attribute the idea to the arguer; whether he or she believes what we have attributed to them. It's clear that in the climate example, someone who expresses the two statements is also committed to the unexpressed assumption that connects them.

The second kind of hidden element involves controversial, even questionable, assumptions that would not be widely accepted by a reasonable audience. This type of hidden component requires support and leaving it unexpressed avoids the obligation of doing so. I say obligation because we want to treat our audiences with the right kind of respect, and that means giving them the information they need to make a reasonable judgment about what we are arguing. If we hide a controversial point, hoping it may go unnoticed, then we are not behaving in the right way toward our audiences (there's an ethics involved here). And, equally important, if it doesn't go unnoticed, then critics will quickly turn the point against us. We will be accused of trying to persuade an audience in an unreasonable manner.

Dr. Tedros' argument, to repeat the point of concern (I think the context justifies repetition here), jumps from an activity that risks the lives of health care workers and those they serve to a claim of "murder." Is that jump reasonable?

Let's consider his argument:

- Premise: health workers working without PPE are risking their lives, and that also risks the lives of the people they serve.
- Sub-conclusion: It is criminal, and it is a murder.
- Conclusion: And it has to stop."

Why does it have to stop? Because it's criminal and murder. Fair enough. There's no problem seeing such a connection given the values that we share. Criminal activity and particularly murder are things we strive to prevent. But to ask a similar "why?" about the claim of murder and see the response as "because health workers are working without PPE" is where the gap arises. We don't obviously see the connection. And if there is no connection, then the premise is not relevant to the sub-conclusion and the argument fails to be reasonable (because it does not follow logically). So, what is Tedros thinking? How does *he* seem to see the connection?

We can look at the background to someone's remarks by reviewing the place where we have found the argument. I took this from the *Hindustan Times*, but it appeared across many media sources. The report actually doesn't provide much more information; but it gives us enough for what we need (a nice example of Grice's maxim of quantity, perhaps). We read that: "Corruption around medical safety gear is tantamount to 'murder', by depriving health workers treating COVID-19 patients of the protection they need, the World Health Organization chief said." Dr. Tedros traces the problem to corrupt authorities who are misusing funds provided to treat COVID-19, and thereby depriving the frontline workers and those they treat of vital materials that they need to protect themselves. That's not a direct report, like the other statements that I used to reconstruct the argument. But indirectly, it shows his thinking. If someone is provided the funds to address an issue with life and death consequences, and they fail to do what they are obligated to do (due to corruption), then they are liable for the negative consequences that follow. In this case, they are liable for deaths of health workers and their patients. In his view, such corrupt officials are murderers, and so the act they perform, or fail to prevent, is murder.

This is controversial and warrants being added as a hidden premise to the argument. We need something like: "If people die because of the corrupt actions of officials not providing PPE, then this is murder." As always when including components of an argument we believe to be hidden, we need to check that it is reasonable to attribute this premise to Dr. Tedros. And, in the circumstances and given what he has said, there seems little doubt that he does believe the suggested statement.

Now, the strength of the argument will depend upon the hidden premise that has been extracted. And that, it needs to be recognized, is the weakest point (which often happens with suppressed controversy). Many people assessing the argument will not judge that the case clearly qualifies as an example of murder or potential murder. Yes, there is liability and criminal negligence. But "murder" is a strong charge, and some will want to know more about the intentions of the accused before they will accept it.

On other hand, the other part of the sub-conclusion states that "it is criminal." And on that front, the corresponding hidden assumption connecting the premise to the statement is much stronger, exactly because we are happier judging the concern as criminal than as murder. "If people die (or are simply put at risk) because of the corrupt actions of officials not providing PPE, then this is criminal." Fewer people will have difficulty accepting this and the argument—as an argument—would have been better with this alone. But Dr. Tedros wanted to make a point, one that he judged was warranted by the circumstances. And it is difficult to second-guess him on that.

7 Argument and explanation (what it all means)

Argument #7

> We should be worried about any virus that explores humans for the first time, because it's overcome the first major barrier. Once inside a cell and replicating, it can start to generate mutations that could allow it to spread more efficiently and become more dangerous.
>
> Jonathan Ball, Jan 20, 2020

We use reasoning to achieve a number of different ends, and much of it is directly argumentative. For example, we try to persuade, we justify our actions, we think through to the better of several outcomes and then choose it, and so forth. We also use reason to offer explanations. Some explanations are straightforward in giving us reasons for what we already know: an accident has occurred, what was the most likely cause? But some explanations are more argumentative because there could be several plausible accounts for something, and we need to decide which is the better. You see the difference when you receive a new piece of furniture that must be assembled. The instructions provided lead you through the process of construction, step by step. That's a clear explanation. On the newscast that day, there's a story of a bridge collapse and various people are interviewed offering reasons for the disaster. Those reasons, if plausible, become hypotheses that will be explored by the investigators as they reason through to the most likely explanation. That's argumentative reasoning of an explanatory nature.

In this piece, virologist Jonathan Ball is explaining to the BBC (reported there and on India TV News) why we should be worried about something. At that time, in the context in which this was being delivered—as a previously unknown virus began to spread across the world in January 2020—the worry was already arising.

DOI: 10.4324/9781003326328-9

Ball was arguing why it was right to be worried and giving reasons for this. At the same time (January 2020), other people were playing down the alarm. They were encouraging people not to worry. So, Ball's explanation takes on more argumentative force in the context. In retrospect, of course, Ball's observations seem prophetic, but he was only explaining the science as it illuminated an unfolding event. Months before the Delta and Omicron variants began decimating communities, the science of mutation is the primary reason given for concern.

Dr. Ball is an expert; he has credentials and experience in a relevant field that makes his argument authoritative. This is why his opinion has been sought out by media sources, hungry for information about something that most people will not understand. You can imagine (and maybe even recall) the thought processes that would have prompted such an interview. "Should we be worried about this new virus which has started to appear?" "Yes, we should." "And why is that?" And so, the explanation proceeds. A claim is given followed by reasons for it. We can reverse the order to see the flow of reasoning:

- Premise: The virus has overcome the first major barrier. Once inside a cell and replicating, it can start to generate mutations that could allow it to spread more efficiently and become more dangerous.
- Conclusion: We should be worried about any virus that explores humans for the first time.

We don't need to retain the "because" here; it's done its job of distinguishing parts of the discourse, separating claim from reasons. In arguments, "because" has the meaning of "for the reasons that"; in explanations, it will often have the meaning of "by the cause of." In our example, because it's argumentative, it's the first sense that is involved.

Most people will not have the background to judge the acceptability of Dr. Ball's reasons. In our day-to-day interactions, we have to trust many people who provide us with important information, and chief among these are experts. I'll consider how to approach expert testimony in Argument #21. For now, we can just recognize its force, standing behind an example like this. If you want to know about viruses, you go to a virologist. And that's what the media sources have done. It's then up to consumers of the media reports to unpack the argument and decide how reliable it is.

Of course, the explanation for caution comes with notable qualifiers: once inside a cell, viruses *can* start to generate mutations that *could* allow it to spread more efficiently and become more dangerous. No guarantees that this will happen, then. But this type of scientific reasoning depends on what has happened in the past. This is how viruses behave. Some have serious outcomes, others less so. But this is enough for us to judge that the caution has reasonable support.

With explanations, we add a third standard of reasoning to the two we have already encountered—deductive and inductive. When we encounter a puzzling situation, we reason through the possibilities associated with it and arrive at one that we think is most likely. In doing so, we have used *abductive* reasoning. The American philosopher Charles Sanders Peirce (1839–1914) coined the term "abduction" as a primary type of scientific reasoning.

You come home and find the door ajar. The first thought that enters your head is that you've been burgled. But then you start to think through other possibilities. It was very windy during the day and the wind may have blown open a door that wasn't properly closed. Somebody in the house was doing the shopping today and may have come into the house carrying a lot of bags and so not closing the door behind them. And so forth. As you review the various possible explanations, you assign different weights of likelihood to each. If you live in a neighborhood with a very high crime rate, then your first impulse may acquire a higher probability.

Depending on who you talk to, abductive reasoning is important for generating hypotheses (Peirce) or evaluating the ones you have generated and deciding on the best from amongst them. That's the way abduction is now understood, as "reasoning (or, inference) to the best explanation." It's not just reserved for scientific reasoning, but is a primary means by which we reason, alone and together, when trying to resolve puzzles.

We can see Dr. Ball's argument as the result of a similar process. We have a puzzle: a new virus has appeared on the scene, so we need to decide how to treat it. We do not know what other possibilities arose for the reasoner here, although one of them would have been to ignore it. But he arrives at the decision that we should be worried about a virus that explores humans for the first time, and the best explanation for such worry is the one he gives. Of course, as the pandemic develops and the virus spreads, that explanation gains more plausibility from experience. And this experience will feed future reasoning on similar issues.

8 Seeing is believing (the power of an image)

Argument #8

Figure 8.1 Breonna Taylor, Louisville Billboards, August 2020. Internet meme.

Our engagement with social media indicates many things about the kind of people we have become, and among those things is how reliant we often are on visuals to acquire and communicate information. Unsurprisingly, this influences the ways we argue. Some people who study these things believe an image can be an argument, others believe that images can provide supplementary material to an argument. That is what we have here. During the Black Lives Matter! Protests of August 2020, billboards sprang up all over Louisville at the instigation of Oprah Winfrey's *O Magazine*. These billboards display a picture of Breonna Taylor and accompanying texts demanding justice for the woman. On March 13th, Breonna was sleeping in her apartment when members of the Louisville Metro Police executed a no-knock search

DOI: 10.4324/9781003326328-10

warrant. Because the officers were out of uniform, another person in the apartment exchanged gunfire with them and Breonna was hit multiple times and killed.

The text supplied on the billboards (26 were put up, one for each year of Breonna's life) advocates for a specific action on the viewer's part: to demand that the officers involved in her shooting be arrested and charged. In support of that is the quote from Oprah Winfrey "If you turn a blind eye to racism, you become an accomplice to it." If correct, that's a compelling reason for performing the action that the claim advises. Assumed here is that *not* demanding justice for Breonna would be turning a blind eye to racism, which involves the further assumption that the killing of Breonna Taylor was a racist act. In the context of the summer of 2020, this was not a difficult assumption to accept in the United States; the killing took its place among too many other similar incidents. And all three of the officers involved were white.

Beyond this issue of importance that captured so much attention in 2020 is its particular relevance to our study of arguments. Because it is different from those we have already seen and will continue to see in this book. It involves an image, and that image may play a role in any force the argument has. What is that role, and what role might images generally play in arguments?

For many people, this is a controversial issue. They see arguments as essentially linguistic entities involving propositions. An argument, *by definition*, is a set of propositions related in such a way that one serves as a claim concluded from others (at least one other, and maybe more). That's non-negotiable for those who take a traditional approach to arguments. Moreover, some will insist here that we are speaking of truth propositions. That is, the conclusion of an argument is either true or false, and our evaluations ought to be able to determine which is the case. Other scholars call this kind of thinking "linguistic imperialism," and insist that just because this is the way arguments have been taught and understood, that doesn't mean it is the only way they are expressed. Or, more controversially, that there are non-linguistic arguments. The example we have walks the line between these two extremes, mixing words and image for a combined effect. So, ultimately, traditionalists will be happier with such an example because they can focus on the linguistic element to extract the argument. But we might still ask whether the choice of image adds something to the argument which cannot be reduced to propositions. Because that is what proponents of the study of visual arguments claim.

While this is the only example in the current collection that involves an image, the issue returns when we look at one that is conveyed through a gesture (Argument #11), and it recurs in other non-traditional means of arguing like the use of narratives. It really is a question of whether if something is to be an argument it must be reducible to propositions. Or, whether something argumentative can be accomplished by choosing a mode of expression that is non-traditional.

Besides, there's an assumption in the traditional prejudice of the argument-as-propositions position that while images are difficult to convert to arguments, such is not the case for propositions. Surely, we simply mean what we say? Well, the amount of misunderstanding that arises on a regular basis would count against this. As one of the proponents of visual arguments (Georges Roque) points out, we also apply a complex process of translation when we construct arguments with propositions:

> first, it is necessary to convert words into a sentence, second, the sentence into a proposition, and finally we need to structure the propositions into an argument. So, it would be inaccurate to consider the translation process as unique to images, since there is a comparable translation that takes place with words.

We might be confused by the difference suggested between sentences and propositions, and there is some disagreement among philosophers as to how they should be distinguished. But they are not the same: we can express the same proposition in very different sentences, and while propositions are logical things (true or false), that's not the case for all sentences. Sentences have a looseness to them as they are used in everyday language.

The upshot of Roque's observation is to, minimally, bring verbal arguments and visual arguments onto a level playing field. Neither has any prior claim to superior status such that one sets the standards by which the other should be identified and assessed. And that's what's at issue here. In suggesting that an image should be recast or "reduced" into propositions in order to qualify as an argument, one's understanding of "argument" is given priority. This may not be fair, although I hardly have the space or interest to pursue that here. It's something for you to consider, and I offer some sources in the back of the book to encourage that consideration. The discussion becomes particularly interesting when an example of a visual argument is offered that has no accompanying text. But that, as I've said, is not the case here.

One type of argument that has led to some people taking visual arguments seriously is the advocacy argument. Advocacy arguments do not involve propositions that are true or false, at least not the conclusions. They tell us what we "ought" to do or "should" support. On such occasions, we do not just use arguments to assert truths; we also use them to change an audience's attitudes or behavior. But such things (attitudes and so forth) do not have a truth value. That we *ought* to treat people who are different from us with respect is not true or false, it's a judgment we agree with or not, and we expect reasons to support the claim in making our judgment. It would follow that not all verbal arguments are propositional (unless we want to say that advocacy arguments and other arguments promoting actions are not arguments at all).

Images can also operate as "visual flags." They arrest our attention, calling out to us in a quite personal way. Seeing an image of the young woman who was Breonna Taylor brings her tragedy home in a more immediate way. It didn't just happen to some woman in Louisville, it happened to that woman up there on the billboard (and now, throughout the internet). If she happens to look like you or someone you know, then that brings the argument home with more force. The image finds and captures its audience. This is something propositions alone cannot do.

The billboard argument is relatively simple: it is an advocacy argument. It is asking or inviting its audience to demand that the police officers involved in Taylor's death be arrested and charged. That's the claim. And why should the audience do this? As we saw above, because if someone turns a blind eye to racism, they become an accomplice to it. I have agreed that that's a controversial claim, and that it also includes an equally controversial assumption that Taylor's killing was an act of racism, or the result of it. But I am interested here in how the argument is intended to work, rather than problems some audiences may have with it. I am interested in how the components work together to say what they say. Those statements on the billboard are not the complete argument. They are further supported by the image of a young woman wearing a Louisville EMS shirt (she was a medical worker), adding to the force of the argument in ways I suggested above. She was an important and valued member of the community, as the image shows; she was a young black woman, as the image shows. She was just like many of the people looking up at her on the billboard, as the image shows.

Images have argumentative force. And in the appropriate contexts, they can play important roles in how we argue.

9 Moral argument (what is fair?)

Argument #9

> Ottawa's proposal to separate COVID-19 vaccine for Indigenous people is "unfair" [because] there would be the least amount available in Manitoba …This puts Manitobans at the back of the line. This hurts Manitobans, to put it mildly.

In 2020, Brian Pallister was premier of the Canadian province of Manitoba. In that role, he had a duty to advocate for the interests of Manitobans. All Manitobans. This argument from December 2020 conveys his response to the Canadian federal government's (Ottawa's) decision to allocate vaccine to the provinces and separately to Indigenous populations. Pallister complains of unfairness, presumably in the hope that things may be revised.

We have first to understand the thinking that motivates the charge of unfairness, because it is not obvious from the argument as expressed. The Canadian government planned to distribute vaccines according to population, but also to ensure Indigenous populations received separate allotments. Manitoba has the highest proportion of Indigenous peoples among provinces. So, once the government held back the portion committed to Indigenous people, there would be fewer doses available to "Manitobans" than to people in other provinces. The unfortunate assumption in Pallister's remarks, and the reason for my scare quotes around "Manitobans," is that the Indigenous people of that province are, of course, also Manitobans. The premier of the province, in this argument, suggests otherwise. Perhaps there is another way to understand the proposal to distribute vaccines between provinces and between Indigenous and non-Indigenous populations. And perhaps there is sense in which the province would receive fewer. But in the way the argument is expressed, the attention naturally shifted to the assumption Pallister was making.

DOI: 10.4324/9781003326328-11

Within a day, Indigenous leaders had criticized Pallister's comments, calling them divisive. They had recognized what he had not, that a Manitoban is a Manitoban, regardless of race.

In Argument #6, we looked at the ways reasons can be hidden, how assumptions work below the surface in argumentation. They can constitute what are called "hidden" premises ("hidden" rather than "missing" because they are there and simply need to be drawn out). We have another instance of that here. We cannot get from Pallister's claims about Manitoba being at the back of the line to his assertion that the government's proposed distribution of vaccine is unfair without assuming that somehow the Indigenous population of that province don't count (or don't count equally) as Manitobans. If Manitoba has the highest proportion of Indigenous peoples, and they are served by the policy, then that doesn't necessarily mean Manitobans are hurt. But it may mean that non-Indigenous Manitobans get a lesser amount of the available vaccine than non-Indigenous populations of other provinces. And that is the problem.

So, what is fair? Arguments are a powerful vehicle for promoting social justice, for bringing cases of unfairness to the attention of those who can do something about it. But "fairness" is a vague concept, comparable in its vagueness to concepts like "freedom" and "democracy." Everyone thinks they know what these mean, but few people share a clear understanding. That is why these concepts underlie debates in society. We may say in terms of shared values that most of us would accept the principle that "It is wrong to treat people unfairly." But how that principle would be activated in any particular case is an occasion for clear and careful argumentation.

We are in the domain here of ethical argumentation, where what is in question is not some fact about the world—what *is* the case—but some value that should be promoted—what *ought* to be the case. Fairness is such a value; Pallister's appeal to what is unfair is an instance of this. But we may suspect that what he takes to be unfair would not be shared by other parties involved in the issue. Indeed, the chiefs of Manitoba's Indigenous peoples indicated as much in their criticisms of his position. At issue is the difference between descriptive claims (that describe the world) and prescriptive claims that prescribe how it ought to be.

Some people may dispute whether values are an appropriate subject for arguments. Isn't it just a matter of how we feel, or what we would prefer? Another way to approach this is to ask whether we can move from what *is* the case to what *ought to be* the case? Some professional philosophers would see such a move as fallacious. They claim we cannot move from an "is" to an "ought". In practice, we do give reasons for our moral views (just different kinds). Whenever we regret something that has occurred, we are effectively replacing an "is" with an "ought", at least in our minds. And we will often argue for this. When we read that a child has been tortured and abused in some way, or that companies have knowingly introduced pollutants into the environment when they could have avoided doing so, or that someone's view has been dismissed because of their race or gender, and we shake our heads at these things, then we disagree with what has happened. We would prefer to live in a society in which these things did not occur, and we believe they violate our sense of justice or fairness. When we move to express that disagreement in reasoned statements, then we are arguing for values.

This, of course, was what Pallister was doing. He judged a situation to be unfair and spoke up accordingly. His argument expresses that response. He undoubtedly believes he is offering a strong moral argument, because he has identified unfairness and calls for it. His notion of what is fair, implicit in what he says, involves equal distribution of available resources.

The Canadian government's proposal was based on the identification of four priority groups that were to be the first to receive vaccines (in December of 2020, high numbers of vaccines were not expected to arrive in Canada until the early months of 2021): residents and staff of long-term care facilities, people over the age of 80, front-line health care workers and members of First Nations. Each of these groups was deemed to be particularly vulnerable to infection. So, from the government's point of view, it was never a matter of equal distribution, but of distribution according to need.

Pallister himself said things that recognized the need to protect Indigenous communities. But his reasoning remained controversial because he continued to see a line between Indigenous communities in his province and Manitobans. *That*, in some minds, was judged unfair, because it failed to give equal consideration to all concerned. It relied on a division that so many advocates had struggled to erase. On these terms, the effect of Pallister's controversial assumption renders at least one of his statements incorrect. When he insists the federal government's policy "puts Manitobans at the back of the line," he fails to recognize the ways the policy addresses the needs of all Manitobans, including those who are Indigenous.

Arguments allow us to work with difficult concepts like "fairness" that reflect strong differences of opinion within society. By exploring the reasoning that goes into such arguments, we are able to think more clearly about the different ways such a concept can be understood and used. But careful argument assessment also exposes problematic ways that assumptions about such common values can hide beneath the surface of our reasoning, providing an invisible influence on what we say and how we think.

Part II
Rhetorical argumentation

10 Arguing in silence (the power of a pause)

Argument #10

> The president's counsel also notes that Vice President Biden appeared to have a conflict of interest when he undertook an effort to remove the Ukrainian prosecutor general. If he knew of the exorbitant compensation his son was receiving from a company actually under investigation, the vice president should have recused himself. While ignoring a conflict of interest is not a crime, it is surely very wrong. With regards to Hunter Biden, taking excessive advantage of his father's name is unsavory, but also not a crime. Given that in neither the case of the father nor the son was any evidence presented by the president's counsel that a crime had been committed, the president's insistence that they be investigated by the Ukrainians is hard to explain other than as a political pursuit.
>
> Mitt Romney, February 2020

During February 2020, President Trump suffered the first of two impeachment trials that would mar his presidency. At that time, Republican Mitt Romney defended his decision to vote in favor of impeachment before the Senate. It was clearly a difficult experience for him, but we'll get to that.

Argument #10 is all about the negative side of communication: staying silent; hinting at a premise to be inferred; and drawing a conclusion on the absence of evidence. Romney is exhibiting the last of these strategies in the excerpt above. The argument specifically addresses the second of three defenses that had been presented by the president's team. In Romney's words, this defense was "that the Bidens' conduct justified the president's actions." Romney agrees that if then Vice-President Biden had been aware his son "received exorbitant compensation," then he should have recused himself.

DOI: 10.4324/9781003326328-13

But "in neither the case of the father nor the son was any evidence presented by the president's counsel that a crime had been committed." Romney is assuming, reasonably, that if such evidence existed, the president's team would certainly have presented it. Their failure to do so thus serves as an indication that the evidence did not exist.

Drawing a conclusion on the basis of the *absence* of evidence is often controversial and sometimes fallacious. People may insist we should always use positive evidence to support a position. But the kind of reasoning that Romney displays here is common in law courts (when the failure to prove someone guilty is taken in favor of their innocence) or in the science laboratory (where the absence of evidence against a hypothesis is taken as support for it). Importantly, in cases from law courts and laboratories, the claim must follow from a concerted effort to find the necessary evidence. That's what the trial is all about, after all. So, this effort stands as the key difference between reasonable and unreasonable instances of the argument we are considering. Did the president's legal team make a concerted effort to find evidence against the Bidens? Romney assumes they did, and so might we. The very context of the impeachment trial supports this judgment. The president's team would have welcomed anything that supported the president's case, and this would certainly have followed. In the absence of this, Romney concludes that they have no evidence and so the president's insistence that the Bidens be investigated by the Ukrainians must have been motivated by something else. Romney judges that "something else" to be political. And this supports the case for impeachment and for Romney's position.

Another important feature of this argument comes very early in Mitt Romney's speech. Forty-eight seconds in, by way of presenting his character, he says: "As a senator-juror, I swore an oath before God to exercise impartial justice. I am profoundly religious. My faith is at the heart of who I am. I take an oath before God as enormously consequential." Essentially here he is giving notice that he will place his obligations to God above his obligations to the Republican Party; that his moral commitments compel the action he has chosen (to vote for impeachment). The remarks give the foundations for this position. But the transcript alone fails to convey the power of his performance itself; one sentence simply follows another. In the video, there is a ten-second pause between "My faith is at the heart of who I am" and "I take an oath before God as enormously consequential." A ten-second pause is surprisingly long for an audience watching and waiting. During it, we see a man clearly struggling to maintain his composure, as if the ramifications of what he has just said are pressing on him. And that pause allows an echo of the words that have been spoken, and an indefinable repetition hangs in the air. The audience is drawn back to also dwell on what was said and weigh its significance. This pause makes a difference to the argument. People who first read the transcript and then watch the video agree that the difference is important, even as they struggle to say what it is.

One of the more emphatic uses of the pause was that of Emma Gonzalez at the March for Our Lives Rally in 2018 following the shooting at Stoneman Douglas Highschool in Parkland, Florida, in which 17 people were killed. She extended her "speech" on the platform to coincide with the time it had taken for the shooter to carry out his actions: "Since I came out here, it has been 6 minutes and 20 seconds. The shooter has ceased shooting and will soon abandon his rifle." But most of the time she stood in silence, much to the growing discomfort of her audience and the event's organizers. If ten seconds seems long to pause in a communication, one that extends for minutes can seem an eternity. Staying silent certainly captures another aspect of the negative approach to arguments. But it needs to be a meaningful silence.

Another argumentative pause in June of 2020 was provided to the media by Canadian Prime Minister Justin Trudeau. In a scrum with reporters, Trudeau was asked what he thought of President Trump's recent threat to use the US military against Americans who were protesting as part of Black Lives Matter events. For 21 seconds Trudeau simply stood pondering the issue as if he was searching for a way to answer. But many people in the media interpreted it as a very real answer. In *Kamloops This Week*, for example, editor Chris Foulds wrote: "The silence was deafening and served to send an obvious message… the third of a minute of hush was his response, a definitive rebuke to all things Trump." We may contest the obviousness of this message. Trudeau's own father had found the need to invoke the War Measures Act in Quebec during his time as prime minister. Perhaps Trudeau junior was pondering how to remark on Trump's actions without implying a comment on his own father. But Foulds' reaction was a common one, judging the pause to represent a clear negative judgment on Trump.

Is it reasonable to convey one's own discomfort and thereby make others uncomfortable? Each of the arguers I have mentioned here has her or his own goals in mind, whether it's to stimulate an appropriate emotional reaction that might lead to action, or to condemn another's actions by deliberately contravening the conventions of a news conference and delaying an answer. But the principal argument at issue here is by Mitt Romney, so we should look to that in answering this question.

Romney's pause is an arresting picture of emotional turmoil that the transcript of the speech fails to capture. It is witnessed by his immediate audience in the Senate, and those watching on media (then and subsequently). It is a challenge to others to look at their own motives for acting as they do, without directly questioning those motives. It is a defense of one man's position that in turn invites others to reflect on their own positions. What first appear as statements establishing character can be seen to have the wider result of encouraging others to reflect on their character. If that is an uncomfortable experience, then so be it.

11 What's in a gesture? (racism in an act of dismissal)

Argument #11

"It was this brazen act of one MP [Member of Parliament] to not just say no but to say no loudly and to kind of gesture like this," Singh said later, waving his hand like someone trying to brush off a fly.

In that gesture, I saw exactly what has happened for so long. People see racism as not a big deal, see systemic racism and the killing of Indigenous people as not a big deal, see Black people being the subject of violence and being killed as not a big deal, and in the moment I saw the face of racism.

That's what it looks like when someone dismisses the reality that people are going through. And so I had a moment of anger in seeing that.

Jagmeet Singh, June 21, 2020

In June 2020, the leader of one of Canada's Federal political parties, Jagmeet Singh, was ejected from the Canadian parliament for "unparliamentary behavior." What had he done? He had called another MP, one of members of the Bloc Québécois (another opposition party), a racist. That member had voted against a motion that would have addressed systemic racism in the Royal Canadian Mounted Police force (RCMP). This was during a period when the Black Lives Matter movement was getting prominent attention in the media worldwide, with riots taking place in several cities of the United States. It was, in other words, a time when people's sensitivity toward apparent racism was heightened.

What angered Singh in particular was that the member in question had made a dismissive gesture. As reported by the Canadian Broadcasting Corporation (CBC), from which this example is taken, the Bloc member had flipped his hand "like someone trying to brush off a fly." As Singh interpreted that gesture, it was argumentative:

> In that gesture, I saw exactly what has happened for so long. People see racism as not a big deal, see systemic racism and the killing of Indigenous people as not a big deal, see Black people being the subject of violence and being killed as not a big deal, and in the moment I saw the face of racism.

Strictly speaking, the Bloc member had uttered nothing, but he had implicated a lot. His dismissive gesture had clear cultural currency and would be interpreted by anyone in the relevant culture in the same way that it was interpreted by Singh. That is how he (and we) can be confident that the gesture was just that—dismissive. We are used to people "swatting away" a remark, concern, or objection. We do it ourselves. Such gestures are part of our social language.

Gestures illustrate how our understanding of what is relevant extends beyond statements to other means of communicating what is generally known in a community. They belong to the cognitive environments in which we operate and cooperate. They also illustrate what argumentation theorist, Michael Gilbert, calls the *visceral* mode of argumentation.

Understanding argumentation as a subspecies of the general category of human communication, Gilbert identifies three modes of argumentation reflecting conceptually distinct sources beyond the traditional logical mode that I have explored in earlier examples. In addition to modes that capture the emotional and the intuitive, Gilbert's visceral mode captures arguments that "are primarily physical and can range from a touch to classical nonverbal communication, i.e., body language, to force." Gestures fit this mode.

The English philosopher Gilbert Ryle drew attention to this way of communicating when he explored the role that "winking" has in our society (and historian Erwin Panofsky gave a similar account of the meaning involved in lifting his hat as a form of greeting). The simple contraction of an eyelid conveys meaning as a wink depending on how the audience "reads" it. If it is judged deliberate, rather than a simple twitch, then it will be seen as conspiratorial. What is important is the underlying social code that registers the meanings associated with various physical behaviors.

While all gestures communicate, some communicate arguments, and Singh's case shows how this happens. Drawing on cultural

What's in a gesture? (racism in an act of dismissal)   51

meaning, Singh *saw* in the gesture of his parliamentary colleague an argument for a position he recognized as racist. That is, he saw a dismissal of any need or willingness to treat racism in the specific case that Singh had identified in his parliamentary motion. The gesture was a way of implying "this is not an issue of concern." There is a necessary level of interpretation here, and it would be difficult to "reduce" the argument to propositional form (premises and conclusion), but the core meaning is clear and would be recognized by anyone sharing Singh's cultural background.

To say that it would be difficult to "reduce" the argument to propositional form places the gestural (or visceral) mode in a similar category to the image we explored in Argument #8. In both cases there is something more captured in the argumentative situation than might be expressed in a simple premise/conclusion format. Something that would be lost if it was insisted that all arguments must be reducible to such propositional structures. In this instance, the "more" involves the cultural meaning of the dismissive swatting of a hand. Even the description I have had to give it here is not as effective as the actual experience of seeing the gesture would be. But it is because of the social code that informs this meaning that we are able to share something of what Singh experienced when he saw the gesture first-hand.

Arguments, we recall from the Introduction, are found in people rather than in statements separated from the contexts in which they arise and operate. So, if we are interested in finding arguments, we should look at people. Singh's example leads us to take this literally: in cases of social interaction, we look as we listen, because what we see may be part of what is communicated. Think again about the difference between reading the transcript of Mitt Romney's speech in Argument #10 and the experience of watching him deliver that speech. On one level, his pause, with all the emotion that we see gathered in his physical expression, is another instance of the visceral mode.

This is the point we take away from the example: that hearers (or readers) recognize more than the utterance of a discourse, and intentions cannot be limited in that way. By expanding the category of argument to include "non-traditional" reasons, we expand our understanding of the argumentative situation and the sphere of interaction between communicators. The witness testifies that she felt afraid when the accused confronted her. How should we treat that feeling in deciding the intent of the accused? The bakery has had its exhaust vents designed so that the smell of newly baked bread wafts onto the sidewalk. Is that a reason I suddenly decided to buy a loaf on my way home? The GPS indicates that the next road on the left is the fastest route to your destination, but there's a sign at the junction which indicates a sudden elevation in that direction and you're driving a vehicle that struggles so much on hills you fear it won't survive another attempt. How much did the sign convince you to take the longer route? None of these "reasons" are in the propositional form, yet they are an important part of the argumentative situations in which reasoning goes on, for better or worse. Accounts of multi-modal argumentation like Michael Gilbert promotes are serious attempts to accommodate these situations.

Singh declined to apologize for his outburst and was expelled from the parliamentary assembly for the rest of the day. Arguments, and our responses to them, have consequences and Singh was happy to live with his. In the fallout from his exchange and expulsion, a lot of attention was placed on his charge of racism—a serious charge to make, especially in a political context. But little to any attention was placed on the gesture that provoked the response in the first place. We've corrected that here, because gestures do count when it comes to arguing, and in the social codes that bind us we have the resources to deal with them.

12 Say it again (the power of repetition)

Argument #12

> This is a flu. This is like a flu. It's a little like a regular flu that we have flu shots for. And we'll essentially have a flu shot for this in a fairly quick manner.
>
> February 26, 2020 (CNN)

> You can do it. You don't have to do it. I'm choosing not to do it, but some people may want to do it, and that's OK.
>
> (On wearing a mask) April 3, 2020 (CNN)

President Donald Trump is a master of a specific repetitive rhetorical style that is matched to his preferred mode of expression—Twitter messages. These two examples illustrate what I have in mind and are generally reflective of his type of repetitive messaging. Among the constraints of his chosen platform is the restriction of any "tweet" to 280 characters. That is not much, but it seems perfectly matched with Trump's preference for the rhetorical figure of parataxis, a figure that involves short, simple clauses arranged independently, often without connectives like "and." As former CEO of the *New York Times*, Mark Thompson observes in his study of political language: "Donald Trump's style of parataxis is almost infinitely compressible, as his intuitive mastery of the micro-rhetorical world of Twitter shows." Trump's experiences on this platform encourage a general preference for the type of utterances he uses, matching them to the brief "sound bites" that interviews and media scrums necessitate and the Twitter messages that he can control.

Along with the paratactic clauses there is a pronounced use of repetition. Together, these strategies tell us something about how Trump envisages his audience. A study in 2018 by Chinese scholars Yaqin Wang and Haitao Liu indicates the reading level of Trump's language to be close to a fifth-grade level of education. That is low.

Consider what is involved in the chosen examples: First, speaking of the Coronavirus, the President said: "This is a flu. This is like a flu. It's a little like a regular flu that we have flu shots for. And we'll essentially have a flu shot for this in a fairly quick manner." The repetition of the word "flu" with little variant in meaning serves to provide emphasis. There is no doubt about the subject of the message and the way it is being described. While many politicians are accused of obfuscating language, Trump aims for simplicity. On wearing a mask, Trump writes: "You can do it. You don't have to do it. I'm choosing not to do it, but some people may want to do it, and that's OK." Here, it's a clause that is repeated, "do it" or "to do it." In each of these examples, the short clauses and repetition of terms suggest the speaker (or writer) is "talking down" to an audience in the way one might address children, repeating things for emphasis, trying to avoid misunderstanding through simplicity.

The use of repetition in these examples is also accessible and inviting in important ways. The repeated words and phrases tug the ear and create a familiar tone while aiding the recall that memory requires. The author of an ancient source book of such arguments—the *Rhetorica ad Herennium*—claims that the persuasive effect of the rhetorical figures of repetition arises from "an elegance which the ear can distinguish more easily than words can explain." In such a remark, although written so long ago, I believe there is anticipation of contemporary work on language and neuroscience. As American rhetorician Jeanne Fahnestock observes, in a comment that supports this attention: "Many of the formal devices identified in rhetorical stylistics have been given psychological reality in brain research, providing mutual ratification." Indeed, repetition appears as the deepest and most sustained of neurocognitive patterns accompanying humans through all stages of life, from the infant's babbling to the speech behaviors of dementia. This may go some way to explaining not just the popularity of Trump's rhetorical style, but its effectiveness.

Scholars lay stress on the complex cognitive processes involved in human memory and the ways repetition acts as its engine, and they draw on research that suggests how literary repetition in particular activates the nervous system's learning response.[1] And yet repetition triggers not just recognition of what has been said but also of what is to come, it sends the brain both backward in recovery and forward in anticipation. A famous case will illustrate this: The English theologian William Paley employs it to underline the principal claim of his *Natural Theology*, published in 1802. He constructs his sentences so as to activate the mind to follow a sequential order of the ideas:

> Design must have had a designer. That designer must have been a person. That person is God.

Assuming a prior familiarity with this type of language pattern, someone hearing or reading the passage anticipates the progress that it invites from design to designer, designer to person. Fahnestock enlists research that suggests parallels between listening or reading a text and activations in the brain to promote a neurocognitive explanation for such predictability. In like manner, we might expect brain studies could also show how the rhetorical figure not only carries the mind forward in this way, but also upward toward the climax, from designer to person to God.

Trump's minimalist style is not just repetitive, it is also rhythmic in the extreme. That is part of its attractiveness. Mark Thompson had noted this in his early analyses of the 2016 political campaign. He draws attention to a speech in which the bricks in the wall that Trump wants to build between the United States and Mexico are represented by the letter "w": "... we have to build a wall, folks. We have to build a wall. And a wall works. All you have to do is go to Israel and say how is your wall working? Walls work" (the underlining is Thompson's). There is powerful alliteration here and a rhythmic intensity that would make many poets proud. In his commentary on this, Thompson allows that we cannot be sure just how impromptu or how prepared this is. "It's off-the-cuff, or at least intended to be heard as such—the last thing Donald Trump wants is for his audience to think he is reading from a prepared script." Indeed, the paratactic clauses imitate conversational utterances, independent and yet related.

Let me sum up all these points with a final example (from many more that could be chosen) from a Donald Trump press conference in which he is addressing the situation in the stock market (November 24, 2020):

> I just want to congratulate everybody. The stock market, Dow Jones Industrial Average just hit 30,000, which is the highest in history. We've never broken 30,000, and that's despite

everything that's taken place with the pandemic. The stock market's just broken 30,000 — never been broken, that number. That's a sacred number, 30,000, and nobody thought they'd ever see it.

It is not just the fourfold repetition of the number 30,000 and the twice-stated "stock market" that marks this discourse, there is also the associated phrases "highest in history," "never been broken" (repeated), "nobody thought they'd ever see it" all effectively making the same point. They are all delivered in short, punchy sentences, rattled off here like ticker tape at the Stock Exchange. Cultural historian Walter Ong once observed, "redundancy, repetition of the just-said, keeps both speaker and the hearer surely on the track." And here, we have all the identifying features of Trump's effective, minimalist style. The examples I have used show a consistency of style from 2016 to 2020. It served him well and gave him access to an audience that represented his "base," just as they found through his stylistic choices access to him. As a rhetorical style, it has all the indications of deliberate, conscious invention. It is designed to achieve things that other types of discourse may not be so effective in providing, and it matches the chosen vehicle best available to convey it.

As an argumentative strategy, Trump's use of repetition and parataxis packages arguments in neat, short, memorable sound bites. Easy to grasp, recall, and understand. His tweet on the wearing of masks, sets out the options, indicates his own choice, and authorizes the reader to make the same choice, if they so desire. He recognizes his status as a model for others' decisions and he responds to that: "You can do it. You don't have to do it. I'm choosing not to do it, but some people may want to do it, and that's OK." But he does present the issue as a matter of personal choice and not a public health concern. In that sense, the authorization to perhaps do as he does will seem irresponsible to his critics, given the leadership role that he's expected to take. But there's the argument (this is a choice like any other choice; it's up to you how you decide), and there's the way that argument is delivered, in the minimalist rhetorical style. It is the delivery that has interested me here, because it brings to light something about Trump's relationship with his audience, and it may go some way toward explaining the success of his messages. Because arguments are not just about what is said; it can also matter how it is said. And saying it several times doesn't seem to hurt.

Note

1 Jeanne Fahnestock observes the ancient bonding of rhetorical and literary stylistics, of which contemporary literary theory seems now to have lost sight. "From a rhetorical perspective," she writes, "all texts construct and distort in pursuit of effects. Hence a sharp dichotomy between...the literary and the functional is simply not salient in the rhetorical tradition."

13 Argument and satire (what do we do with the children?)

Argument #13

> Schools are a very appetizing opportunity. I just saw a piece in The Lancet arguing the opening of schools may only cost us 2 to 3% in terms of total mortality...any life is a life lost, but... that might be a trade-off some folks would consider.
>
> Dr. Oz

Dr. Mehmet Oz is a well-known "celebrity health expert," who has offered advice on just about any real or potential ailment that could befall us. So, it was only to be expected that he would make some comment on the pandemic when he appeared on Sean Hannity's show in April of 2020. But what he said more than raised a few eyebrows; it resulted in a considerable backlash. Because Dr. Oz was seen to say that the loss of 2–3% of school children (which would actually amount to hundreds of thousands) was a reasonable price for the presumably greater benefit of opening schools. He is referring to a piece in *The Lancet*, a reputable journal of science research produced in the United Kingdom but consumed across the world. The article in question had referred to a study which found that *closing* schools in the United Kingdom would reduce deaths by 2–4%. So, Dr. Oz is both transposing the results of a study that looked at the context in the United Kingdom to the context in the United States, assuming they are analogous, and shifting from a case for closing schools to opening them. There are problems in the analogy, but that kind of reasoning is explored elsewhere. Our concern here is with what he seems to have inferred from the study, or the judgment he attached to that inference: that the loss of a small percentage of children was acceptable.

Did he really mean that? It's what he said, but what did he mean? A few days later, he apologized, saying he realized his comments

DOI: 10.4324/9781003326328-16

had confused and upset people. He went on to explain that he had misread the study in question, and the losses involved were total numbers that would include parents, friends and family, and not just children. But a more charitable reading of his remarks is that he was using satire, but he now realizes his audience would not see that and so he declines to mention it. Why confuse people more than you already have?

What suggests a satirical reading to me is the even stranger remark at the beginning (one passed over by the critics): "Schools are a very appetizing opportunity." What does the reference to "appetizing" suggest to you, because on the face of things, it doesn't seem to belong here?

Someone else who got in serious trouble for making a suggestion about how children should be treated was Jonathan Swift, that 18th-century Anglo-Irish writer best known for fictional works like *Gulliver's Travels*. But Swift was also a satirist and he used satire to draw people's attention to issues of concern. One of his best-known satirical pamphlets was *A Modest Proposal*, which suggested that one way to address extreme poverty in Ireland was to have the rich eat the children of the poor. Satire uses often humorous or horrifying ideas as a means of criticizing the prevailing attitudes or the way people are behaving. It will often involve irony, that is, it will say the opposite of what the author actually intends. So, satire and irony can be powerful ways to argue.

The reason I take a charitable approach to Dr. Oz's argument and read it as satire is because the mention of "appetizing" in relation to children recalls Swift's suggestion that the rich eat the children of the poor. Perhaps it is a stretch, but it paints Dr. Oz in a kinder light and, most importantly, it provides an opportunity to explore the role of satire in argumentation.

Yet, whatever Dr. Oz's intentions were, his choice of argument in this case was unwise. If you are going to use satire (or irony, or basic allusion), you must expect or ensure that your audience will "get it." That they won't take the literal meaning of what you say to be the actual meaning. This is what makes satirical or ironic argument so challenging. It is not something to be used carelessly, if you want to be understood and avoid the kind of backlash that was experienced in this case.

What can an audience be reasonably expected to see? There are rich sources of narratives and examples available in any society, ranging from the fairy tales we are told as children to the memorable events of history that can acquire a meme status in our media streams. Allusion depends on such a common fund of ideas, images, and stories. And both satire and irony depend on allusion. When you allude to something, you make reference to it indirectly. Perhaps you show someone one thing with the strong belief that it will cause them to think of another thing. When a magazine article refers to a celebrity's "Cinderella past," you know she is another "rags to riches" story. You can fill in the details, as it were, without any more information. The allusion is strong. Or when critics of certain European countries' open acceptance of Syrian refugees fleeing the war in their homeland published cartoons with large wooden horses packed with people (perhaps a Syrian flag on the side to support the allusion) standing before a castle where a recognizable caricature of a European leader was opening the doors, viewers recognized the reference to the Trojan Horse. And the allusion supported the suggested argument that, just as the wooden horse was a threat to Troy and should not have been allowed in, so these refugees represent some (unmentioned) threat to Europe and should not be let in.

Neither the Cinderella nor the Trojan Horse example is satirical or ironic, but this just indicates the greater role that allusion can play in communicating ideas and conclusions. It's also the case that some memes have greater currency than others. A reference to the Trojan Horse may be a sure bet in societies for which this story was part of their education (or, given the Hollywood version, part of their cultural upbringing). A reference to something like Swift's proposal is more tenuous. There was a time when most educated people knew it and would probably catch an allusion; but such a time is not the present. This shows that satire is time-sensitive as well as culturally situated. As an argumentative strategy, satire has long been an important choice for writers living under repressive regimes.

Modern-day satire uses humor to show the weak or bad qualities of a person or policy. British author Ian McEwan gave a prime example of such writing in his novella *The Cockroach* (2019), in which a cockroach wakes up one morning to discover that overnight he has transformed into a human being. And not just any human being, but the Prime Minister of Britain. In this role he oversees a policy of "Reversalism," whereby states aim to reverse their money flow, and in the process somehow improve their economies. McEwan's fiction is a satirical argument undermining the policy of Brexit and ridiculing one of its principal architects, Boris Johnson. But it also depends upon a literary allusion to Franz Kafka's *Metamorphosis*,

Argument and satire (what do we do with the children?) 61

in which a man turns into a giant insect. Satire never loses its argumentative force if it is well constructed and clearly signaled to its audience.

Granting the possibility that Dr. Oz was being satirical, what might his argument have been? What could he have been trying to say in this way that he couldn't say directly? It would be critical of some group or policy, because that is what satire does, it criticizes. Let's review the argument:

> Schools are a very appetizing opportunity. I just saw a piece in The Lancet arguing the opening of schools may only cost us 2 to 3% in terms of total mortality...any life is a life lost, but... that might be a trade-off some folks would consider.

We proceed on the assumption that, just as Swift didn't actually think the rich should eat the children of the poor, so Dr. Oz doesn't think the loss of 2–3% of school children is a reasonable trade-off. Some people (some folks) were pushing for a reopening of schools, presumably on the grounds that education is important and children were being harmed by its loss. Dr. Oz is drawing attention to the possible consequences of such reopening and using the *Lancet* study as support. Starkly put:

> if schools are reopened, then according to a study in The Lancet [here's the support for the consequence] there could be a loss of 2 to 3% of school children. Some people might consider that a reasonable tradeoff...But come on, really? So, schools should not be reopened.

This now says the opposite of what Dr. Oz actually said. But we are not interested in what he said as much as what he meant, or what he can be taken to have meant. The difference hinges on what can be taken to be reasonable. On my reading, Dr. Oz is being critical of anyone who would propose putting percentages of children at risk, and he uses satire to make his point. Some people are so extreme in their reactions that they would accept such an outcome, but they are wrong to do so. And phrasing matters in the way he does, he brings that wrongness into stark relief.

I admit that my reading is controversial, and someone may object to it by insisting Dr. Oz actually meant what he said. Reading the comments on the media sites where his remarks were reported, that's the majority opinion. But that's the point with satire or irony.

It can be taken literally, but that will usually issue in some strange (even absurd) results. My reading reclaims Dr. Oz's argument from that fate.

Satirical arguments are a small and dangerous breed. We employ them at our peril because misunderstanding is so prevalent even in the best of times. When we invite misunderstanding, we should not be surprised by the response. But on those rare occasions when we judge satire might work—when the issue warrants severe criticism and we are confident our audience will catch the allusion and thus see our intention—then satire is a powerful tool of social commentary and political argumentation.

14 Turning the tables (who would be worse?)

Argument #14

> If we have four more years of Trump's climate denial, how many suburbs will be burned in wildfires? How many suburban neighborhoods will have been flooded out? How many suburbs will have been blown away by superstorms?
>
> Joe Biden, September 20, 2020

The 2020 US presidential race was even nastier than past campaigns, if such is possible. Both Donald Trump and Joe Biden spent as much time criticizing the records and abilities of their opponent as they did promoting their own agendas.

Forest fires in California forced hundreds of thousands of people from their homes, destroyed communities and caused a number of fatalities. President Trump seemed to attribute the problem to poor forest management, rather than the climate change that his opponent saw at work. Trump insisted, "When trees fall down after a short period of time, they become very dry — really like a matchstick. And they can explode. Also leaves. When you have dried leaves on the ground, it's just fuel for the fires."

But more to the point here (given how Biden expresses his remarks), Trump had made a point in his campaign of identifying Biden as a threat to the suburbs. On several occasions, he had made comments along the lines that Biden "would destroy the beautiful suburbs" and shatter "your American Dream." On this front, the suburbs are an issue, and the question is posed: who is the greater threat to the suburbs? Trump had suggested it was Biden. In the excerpt above, Biden turns the remark back upon Trump and claims that he (Trump) is the one who is threatening the suburbs).

I say he "claims" this, but, of course, what he provides is a series of questions. But these are what we call "rhetorical questions."

64   *Rhetorical argumentation*

Usually, a question is inviting an answer that is not known. The inquirer genuinely seeks a response. But when a question is rhetorical, the asker already knows the answer. It is stated as a question because the speaker assumes the answer is obvious and it invites the audience to agree with that judgment. Biden is not really asking how many suburban neighborhoods will have been flooded out; he is *asserting* that many neighborhoods will be flooded if Trump is returned. And, again, he is asserting that many suburbs will be burned by wildfires.

Of course, there is something of the playground spat in all this: "you're worse"; "no, you're worse!" But, after all, the playground is one of the places where we learn to argue as part of our socialization. It's just to be hoped that we get better at it as we age, or mature.

And indeed, this strategy of argument is a popular and useful one. If someone is accusing you of something that you believe they have been guilty of themselves, then it's natural to say as much, thereby exposing an inconsistency. Biden is doing more than this; he is taking the force of Trump's criticism about the danger Biden poses to the suburbs and turning it back on him. It's a form of counterargument, like that which we saw earlier in this book. But it has a character of its own.

Much of the vocabulary we associate with arguments and argumentation has its source in Ancient Greek thought, and this strategy is one of them. The term in question is *peritrope*. It sounds a bit like the more common word "periscope," that we associate with submarines. The periscope turns around, giving the viewer a wide look (scope) of the surroundings. The *peritrope* is a trope (that is, a common literary or rhetorical device) that has the specific character of turning around. In its usage, it applies to the opponent, what that person had tried to apply to someone else. In an example written by the Sophist Gorgias, one person accuses another of madness, but the accused person defends himself by claiming the madness lies with the accuser for making such a claim.

A more modern (and recognizable) example would be one used by Martin Luther King Jr. In his *Letter from the Birmingham Jail*, he was responding to a number of criticisms that had been leveled against him by members of the clergy (his own group). Some of those criticisms he proudly owned. When accused of being an extremist, he agreed but insisted that the real question was what kind of extremist he should be (siding with other "extremists" like Jesus). He responds to the disappointment that white religious leaders have in him by turning the charge of disappointment back on those he calls "white moderates" considering them a great stumbling block in the movement for freedom. He laments

> the white moderate who is more devoted to order than to justice; who prefers a negative peace which is the absence of tension to a positive peace which is the presence of justice; who constantly says, "I agree with you in the goal you seek, but I can't agree with your methods of direct action"; who paternalistically feels that he can set the timetable for another man's freedom; who lives by the myth of time.

A number of these points had received independent responses in the letter. But in these remarks, he turns the criticisms back onto his critics, showing (and admitting) "an unreasonable impatience."

An understanding of context is crucial to recognizing when the tables have been turned. This strategy is invariably used when two or more people are in dialogue with each other or their positions, contesting some claim. So, the background of the exchange needs to be fully appreciated. It is important, for example, to know that Donald Trump had identified Biden as a threat to the suburbs. Thus, Biden's own reference to the suburbs makes sense in that context. Likewise, Trump's skepticism toward claims that climate change was responsible for the Californian fires is needed background for understanding the full target of Biden's comments.

Let's look carefully at the argument in Biden's remarks, taking the assertions out of the questions:

> If we have four more years of Trump's climate denial, many suburbs will be burned in wildfires.
> If we have four more years of Trump's climate denial, many suburban neighborhoods will be flooded out.
> If we have four more years of Trump's climate denial, many suburbs will be blown away by superstorms.

You'll see that I have made adjustments beyond just eliminating the questions. I've repeated the opening refrain (the antecedent), for example. But, I would suggest, there is no question that Biden is committed to each of these statements. This is his position. And so, we can take the three statements as premises for at least the conclusion that "We cannot have [afford] four more years of Trump's climate denial." And, thus, the further conclusion that "Trump cannot be re-elected."

This reading, however, does go as far as the context permits. That is, it doesn't actually capture the identified peritrope. Because in the context of Trump's earlier criticism of Biden, Biden is also saying that "Trump will destroy the beautiful suburbs, not me." Is this fair? In the context, it's also part of Biden's reasoning and supports his position that he would be a better president than Trump.

Fairness will be an issue in judging arguments that turn the tables in this way. It may be objected, for example, that Biden is assuming Trump is wrong about the cause of the California fires and, more importantly, wrong in his beliefs about the impact of climate change. And this assumption might be challenged. So, a much larger controversy over climate science stands behind this argument. Indeed, this is the case, and how an audience member feels about that background issue will likely affect whether they are persuaded by Biden's argument.

It should also be observed—again, in the interests of fairness—that when Trump identified Biden as a threat to the suburbs, he was referring to Biden's approach to crime and his housing policies. When Biden identifies Trump as a threat to the suburbs, he is referring to the negative impact of his environmental policies. So, the two are talking about different things and one response is not relevant to the other. Perhaps. But in a major political campaign like the one in which they were involved, it is very difficult to isolate topics. And drawing these points together, the person concerned for the suburbs could still see themselves being asked to decide whose policies (on the environment, crime, and housing) would be detrimental to the suburbs, if any would.

From our perspective, the 2020 campaign provided us with different argumentative strategies at work and different types of argument. The peritrope was one of them, and so one to watch for in other, similar, situations.

15 Emotional appeal (a call to aid)

Argument #15

Canada has an aging population, and helping the elderly better prepare themselves will protect us all. This is an opportunity for communities to come together and support the vulnerable people who live among us.

Public Health Agency of Canada also suggests neighbors create "a buddy system in which you agree to check in on each other and run essential errands if you become sick" – community support that is essential for older adults living alone.

In the neutral zone between panic and complacency is an opportunity to think about what we can do – and maybe should already have done – to protect ourselves and our loved ones in the future.

March 12, 2020

As COVID-19 started to take hold of people's lives and close down communities in the early months of 2020, there came a growing awareness that some groups were more vulnerable than others. Chief among these groups were seniors, especially those living together in retirement residences. Initially, attention was focused on hospitals and ensuring the needs of the sick and people with comorbidities were addressed. But very quickly it became apparent that greater risks were being experienced among older members of communities. In the first wave, COVID-19 was viewed as an old people's disease because that was where the principal fatalities tended to be seen.

The argument above comes from a larger piece drawing attention to the importance of caring for older adults. The article appeared in a major Canadian newspaper and so had as its intended audience the general population of Canadians. The argument is an appeal for

DOI: 10.4324/9781003326328-18

people to act, and in the context, it is an emotional appeal because it aims to stimulate an emotional reaction in the audience. The writers want people to care about others and transform that care into action. As with Argument #9, there is an ethical dimension to this reasoning (people *should* act), but my interest with this example is the role emotion plays in the argument.

Emotion as a mode of argumentation was mentioned in Argument #11, where the focus was on the visceral mode. Both modes, we will recall, are part of Michael Gilbert's theory of multi-modal argumentation. With this example, we shift our attention to the emotional mode and the place of emotion in argument generally.

For some people appeals to emotions, like pity, raise suspicion. They seem to divert audiences away from reason to consider what is deemed "irrational." So, earlier theorists have raised concerns about the fallacy of appealing to emotion. Indeed, such distraction can occur and can be unreasonable. But is all appeal to emotion unreasonable? Aristotle considered this question when he confronted the way that tragic plays, when performed in the theater, encouraged responses of pity and fear in audiences. These encouragements were deliberate, and he thought they were okay. Pity and fear are natural emotional responses, after all, and we need to appreciate the roles they play in everyday experience. Sometimes, an emotional appeal is an important way to catch our attention and focus it on something that warrants thought and action. Think about the media campaigns that bring famines and other human catastrophes into our living rooms. Not all appeals to pity are fallacious. So, we need to consider what makes a difference between reasonable and unreasonable appeals.

One argumentation theorist who has taken a serious approach to this question is Douglas Walton. Along with several colleagues, he has identified a collection of what he calls "argumentation schemes." These are regular patterns of argument that occur in natural situations. Each scheme is accompanied by a set of critical questions to aid in exploring the potential reasonableness of any particular example. We saw one earlier when I discussed definitions in Argument #5, and we will look at more of these schemes in Part IV of this book because they comprise many common strategies of argument. But here, I want to consider how Walton treats emotional appeals and look at Argument #15 in the light of such a treatment. Walton and his colleagues call the scheme "Emotional Plea: Argument from Need for Help," and they judge that this is a common enough pattern to include it in their compendium of schemes. Indeed, certain circumstances will lend themselves to using such a pattern, and the rise of a pandemic can easily be judged such a circumstance.

As Walton and his colleagues see the pattern, there is a general premise that implicitly captures a sense of obligation, where if a group needs help and another group can give that help, then it should provide that help, assuming it would not be too costly to do so. Another premise identifies the group that needs help and the specific action that could provide it. A further premise then assures us the proposed action would not be too costly for those helping. And then a conclusion is drawn that, given the above, obligates the group to act.

Let's see how this pattern fits the argument we are looking at:

- Premise: For all elderly Canadians and Canadians in general, Canadians in general should help the elderly if they need help and providing it would not be too costly. [Canada has an aging population, and helping the elderly better prepare themselves will protect us all. This is an opportunity for communities to come together and support the vulnerable people who live among us.]
- **Premise**: Elderly Canadians are in a situation where they need help [*c*ommunity support that is essential for older adults living alone].
- **Premise**: Canadians in general can provide community support.
- **Premise**: Providing community support would not be too costly to Canadians in general.
- **Conclusion**: Canadians ought to provide community support to older adults. [*I*n the neutral zone between panic and complacency is an opportunity to think about what we can do – and maybe should already have done.]

Two things will be observed here: first, it doesn't fit the pattern exactly. That's the way with arguments in natural discourse; they often have to be adjusted to fit. The important thing is that a reader or listener can recognize the general strategy of argument that is at stake. In that sense, the example fits this scheme. The second thing to observe is that no mention is made of emotion, other than in the title of the argument pattern. So, where is the emotional appeal? It lies in the motivation to act. It is not a direct appeal to reason *per se*; it is an attempt to identify a vulnerable group that needs specific help because of that vulnerability. It is an attempt to stimulate a response of care and concern and motivate action as a result of that response. Because the focus here is on the act of helping, weighed against the costs of providing help.

Such contextual considerations as these are brought out by the thicker description of the context that turning to some critical questions for appraisal gives us. The pattern itself only provides a thin description. Evaluative questions draw us into the deeper aspects involved in, or implied by, the reasoning. The critical questions for any argument schemes will not automatically tell us if an argument is strong or weak. But they will direct us to the right things to ask so that we can make that judgment for ourselves.

Walton and his colleagues ask three critical questions of any argument that fits the pattern of this scheme: (1) Would the proposed action really help the group that has been identified as needing help? (2) Is it possible for those to whom the appeal is being made to carry out the proposed action? And (3) would there be negative side effects of carrying out the action that would be too costly? I think we can see that it isn't difficult to judge the argument reasonable on these terms. But let's consider each question in turn.

1 The proposed action is providing community support for older adults living alone. And that support is described as a "buddy system" where people check in on each other and run essential errands for those sick. We recognize that this argument is being issued during the opening stages of the pandemic when society (at least Canadian society) was largely under lock-down. People were expected to stay home, and so those who were on their own were essentially isolated. Having someone check on them periodically provided more than just a health check; it provided minimal social interaction, something on which most of us rely for our general well-being. And further, having people run errands for those sick obviously would help the elderly. So, the first critical question is answered in the affirmative. Moreover, recognizing need in this way stimulates an emotion of care. It is part of the emotional appeal involved in this argument.

2 The second question doesn't ask whether people want to carry out the action; it asks whether they can do so. Our obligations often conflict with our desires, pushing us out of our comfort zones. But it's also possible that we might be asked to do something that people, generally, are not in a position to do, like donating large sums of money. In this case, it is difficult to see the action as what ethicists call supererogatory (that is, beyond what is normally expected by one's duty), or even

overly altruistic (where we put another's needs before our own). In fact, the argument suggests there is also personal benefit to those acting because acting this way is deemed to protect people now and in the future. So, the conditions of the second question have also been met.

3   Finally, does the action have costly (or, too costly) consequences for those asked to act? In many cases, this will be the crucial question, just as disagreements are most likely to arise around what is *too* costly. The question recognizes that any action of this type comes with costs, even if they are only those involving an expense of time, as in this case. Altruistic behavior, even at a minimal level, can push people outside of their comfort zones. But it is an important question because it focuses the mind on what someone is prepared to do for others, on how much they see their involvement in a community requiring they commit to that community, and on what they are prepared to sacrifice for the common good. These are not considerations we can answer for each other; they require a deeply personal response to the argumentation involved and depend upon our involvements in the deeper contexts of the issue. As I note, this argument seems to require no more than a commitment of time. Of course, when this argument was published (March 2020), there were many things about the virus that were not understood, and so some people might have felt uncomfortable checking in on someone who could be sick. So, not everyone may have given the same response to the third question.

Overall, this example was an easy fit for the scheme and the questions were not difficult to answer. Other arguments may prove more challenging when viewed through the lenses of the critical questions. What if it is not the elderly during a pandemic who we are being asked to help, but refugees dislodged from somewhere else in the world by a civil war? Or what if it is not running errands that we are being asked to do to help those around us, but becoming vaccinated to minimize the spread of the virus and take pressure off hospitals? These arguments—also involving emotional appeals—have been more controversial, in part because people judge the costs of the action to be greater than their obligations to perform the action, or they challenge whether they even have such an obligation at all. There may be many more of these types of argument going on around us than we previously appreciated.

Part III
Character-based argumentation

16 Praising character (the best amongst us)

Argument #16

> Among the words that best describe Ruth, tough, brave, a fighter, a winner, but also thoughtful, careful, compassionate, honest. When it came to opera, insightful, passionate. When it came to sports, clueless. Justice Ginsburg had many virtues of her own, but she also unavoidably promoted one particular one, humility in others.
>
> Chief Justice John Roberts' speech honoring Ruth Bader Ginsburg (Sept 23, 2020)

We might think a funeral or memorial speech to be a strange place to find an argument. But, recalling Wayne Brockriede yet again, and his insistence that we find arguments in people, where else than in these kinds of discourses might we best find what matters about people, where else might we find the best people? In a brief, five-minute speech, Chief Justice Roberts gave a vivid portrait of the jurist and woman, coloring his comments with anecdotes and details of her career.

Ruth Bader Ginsburg was an associate justice of the Supreme Court of the United States for 27 years. During that time, she wrote several notable majority and dissenting opinions. She was known for her liberal views and as a champion of those who suffered discrimination.

In this section of the book, we turn our attention to the role character plays in Argument. That is, we are specifically interested how people enter into the content of arguments and serve as evidential backing in the support provided for claims. Given the lead of Brockriede, we would expect character to have a considerable role in arguments. And, indeed, in this argument and the next, we will explore the positive role of character.

In the discussion of audiences in Argument #4, I noted three audiences identified by Aristotle. Two of them were audiences as judges, not judges in the sense that Ruth Ginsburg was a judge, but deliberators judging what has happened in the past or what ought to be done in the future. It is the third audience and the corresponding type of genre that is of relevance here, the audience that is often relegated to the margins of discussion because it is thought not to bear the importance of the other two. This is epideictic speech, the type of discourse that we hear on ceremonial occasions when an important event occurs. The loss of a figure like Ginsburg was just such an event in the life of the United States. The primary aim of such speech is to eulogize (or blame) a person, group, or movement, and so forth. It identifies important qualities in its subject and raises that subject as someone or something to be honored and emulated. Epideictic is a discourse that promotes values and, as in this case, uses a person of exemplary character to promote the importance of those values.

When the subject of epideictic is a person, events like funerals, memorials, and award ceremonies are where we are most likely to encounter it. And given how important and frequent such events are in daily life, we can expect to encounter it often. Epideictic speech usually has an element of exaggeration about it, but that's because when we promote values or characters, we naturally elevate them. We figuratively put them on pedestals, and we reach for ornamental language fitting for the task.

What is the argument here in Chief Justice Roberts' memorial address? It doesn't fit easily alongside other pieces I have discussed. There's no clear conclusion standing out, and hence no obvious support for that conclusion. Yet epideictic discourse is argumentative in important ways, and this example illustrates the point.

The speaker is not just talking about the person being honored; he is sorting through all the things that could be said and choosing things which he believes best represents the woman, that best convey a portrait of who she was. And so he looks for words that "best" describe her, and chooses "tough, brave, a fighter, a winner, but also thoughtful, careful, compassionate, honest." Each of these could undoubtedly be elaborated upon and supported with examples from the life. Each conveys something positive. In combination, and balanced as he intends, they start to present a rich and complex picture, to which he will add. Most important is the way this excerpt ends: "Justice Ginsburg had many virtues of her own, but she also unavoidably promoted one particular one, humility in others." He illustrates this by explaining how he learned humility when someone was interested in her opinion rather than his own. But there's more to unpack here. That she had virtues of her own has already been supported with the list of qualities of character he has provided. That is how we understand virtue—as a quality of character. So, being brave is a virtue, as is being compassionate. Humility is a virtue that others learn from being associated with her. That's important here. There's being virtuous, and there's communicating the power of virtue so that it is inculcated in others. That's what Justice Ginsburg did; that's an aspect of her character that is being praised.

So, the argument here is not so very complicated, even though it needs to be reconstructed from what has been said:

> Ruth Bader Ginsburg was a woman of great importance/value/ esteem because she possessed virtues of her own and encouraged virtues in others.

She was an example of how to live, and how to live well. Other people will add to this portrait, as they did on the occasion in question when she laid in state in the great hall of the Supreme Court building. They will speak of her as a champion of justice who taught the importance of treating people fairly and of forgiveness. Collectively, they will contribute to the argument that the occasion invites and, in September of 2020, that the nation may well have needed. It was a time of social divisiveness where justice often seemed in short supply. Holding up an example of what justice can be and do is a fitting way to respond to that moment in time.

Why should we honor character? Because it is one of the ways that virtue is given a public face, literally. Brave people do brave things; compassionate people act compassionately. In each of our lives, certain people stand out as being important for us because of what they have taught us and the values they have conveyed. These may be public figures, but whoever they are, the qualities of character that we valued in them were given public expression, otherwise, we wouldn't be aware of them. In ethical theory, virtues are difficult to appreciate because they are qualities of character and character is essentially hidden inside the person. Other ethical theories can talk of consequences of an action, which are public, or duties which also have a shared accessibility. But virtue is only seen when a person acts, when the type of character she or he has developed influences what that person does. There is an important relationship between who we are and how we act. We can mask who we are on occasion, but over time that is difficult to do.

When Chief Justice Roberts closes with the statement that "she will live on in what she did to improve the law and the lives of all of us," he identifies the kind of legacy that epideictic arguments often support because they have an educative role. In fact, argumentation theorists Chaim Perelman and Lucie Olbrechts-Tyteca argued that there is an important relationship between epideictic speech and education. For them, "the purpose of an epideictic speech is to increase the intensity of adherence to values held in common by the audience and the speaker," and that is often a role shared by the educator. The other two kinds of speeches—the forensic and the deliberative—make use of dispositions already present in an audience. But the epideictic speech can cultivate those dispositions. What this means, besides suggesting that epideictic underlies the other types and increases in importance because of this, is that when we have a disposition to act in a certain way, we are more likely to do so. Exposure to characters like that of Ruth Bader Ginsburg encourages the development of a disposition for, say, compassion. The result, ideally, is more compassion in a community. That's why this type of character argument is significant.

The American playwright, Florida Scott-Maxwell wrote in her own memoir about the importance of claiming the events of your life. "When you truly possess all you have been and done, which may take some time, you are fierce with reality." And when you don't have the opportunity to do this for yourself, it falls to others to do it for you, as Chief Justice John Roberts provides for Ruth Bader Ginsburg. In light of the epideictic argument delivered, I think we can agree that Justice Ginsburg was "fierce with reality."

17 Reflecting values (an excellent choice)

Argument #17

[She is an excellent choice because] she will undo the damage of the Trump administration, restore the department's work force and expertise, uphold our obligations to Native communities, and take the bold action needed to tackle the accelerating climate and nature crises.

                Senator Tom Udall (on Native American Deb Haaland's appointment to the US cabinet)

I do not want to leave the idea that positive character arguments belong primarily in the domain of the funeral speech. Nothing could be further from correct. This argument from New Mexico Senator Tom Udall, is an implicit appeal to the character of Democratic congresswoman Deb Haaland, but without identifying the kinds of virtues or values that we saw in the epideictic argument of #16.

Congresswoman Haaland, a Pueblo of Laguna, was chosen by President Biden to become the first Native American cabinet secretary and one of the first Native Americans appointed to serve in a US cabinet. This move was widely applauded with many supporters focusing attention on what she was. Udall gives his attention to *who* she is. Of course, he didn't ignore her heritage altogether, calling the appointment a "watershed moment for Native communities, and for our nation." But none of the supporting evidence explicitly depends on her Native background (assuming that other secretaries have dealt with US obligations to Native communities).

Appeals to a person are a particular type of argument that fall under the general label of ethotic reasoning. Different types of ethotic arguments are identified as such because they all involve *ethos* in some way. *Ethos* is a Greek word that can also refer to the spirit of a culture. But in argumentation theory, it is taken to refer to an individual's character. The Greeks saw it as an important source of persuasive evidence, along with *pathos* and *logos*. Essentially, it has long been recognized that, for various reasons, people are not always persuaded by strong logical arguments (*logos*). Something (or -things) more needs to contribute to the persuasive force. The arguer might find a way to connect with the audience on an emotional level, stimulating an appropriate response in them. This is the force of *pathos*, awakening *pathé* or passions. We saw this at work in Argument #15. Additional force can come from the person who delivers the argument, as they convey credibility or trust through what they say, that is, as they communicate their character, showing good will or virtuousness. That's the central way in which *ethos* was understood—as a person using their own character in support of what they said.

Now, this sense of *ethos* is expanded in a range of ethotic arguments that may be used by one person to appeal to another person's character. And, as we will see in the next two arguments, it may involve negative attacks on another person's character as a way of making a point or undermining an argument that they have made. So, ethotic reasoning involves a rich set of argumentative strategies available for use.

The argument we are exploring here, appeals to the experience of an individual, noting the various strong points that are brought together in that person's character. Think about how similar reasoning works in employment situations. A group, company, or team is considering adding a member to their work force. They interview various candidates, and then they discuss what each candidate could bring to the job, deliberating about the various qualities each has in terms of experience and abilities. It is such a collection of features that one individual has that ultimately moves that person to the top of the list and the decision makers then conclude that this is the person to hire. They have used ethotic reasoning, but quite different in nature from the way we saw Chief Justice Roberts using such reasoning in praising Ruth Bader Ginsburg.

We can now see that we have reasoning of this kind in the argument we are considering, because Haaland has been chosen from among other candidates. We don't know why she was chosen, because we are not given the argument behind Biden's choice (not here, at least). But we do know why Udall thinks she was a good choice, because he tells us his reasons. She is a good choice because:

Reason 1: She will undo the damage of the Trump administration.

We can expect certain qualities of strength and determination are required here, along with a perceptiveness to understand the current situation and how it can be improved or addressed. Note the controversial hidden assumption here—that the Trump administration damaged the work of the department of the interior, although the very next reason clarifies the first.

Reason 2: She will restore the department's work force and expertise.

Restoring expertise requires the right kind of judgment and the ability to identify knowledgeable people. If Udall did not believe she possessed these qualities, his confidence in her would not be justified.

Reason 3: Uphold our obligations to Native communities.

A sense of duty and the concern to fulfill it is indicated here. Of course, she is well-positioned to address Native communities in a way that earlier holders of the appointment may not have been.

Reason 4: And take the bold action needed to tackle the accelerating climate and nature crises.

The strength and determination behind the first reason are reiterated here. This may be the most difficult part of the portfolio, but Udall sees something in her background to believe she will act with boldness.

The reasons, then, suggest a certain kind of character, with the qualities implicit in the actions he expects her to take. In the last argument (#16), I noted the importance of character to action. Since there is an integral relationship between who we are and what we do, people of a certain kind of character are expected to act a certain way. Conversely, people who act a certain way can be expected to have related qualities of character. None of this is guaranteed, of course, but it explains the attraction of appeals to character.

As I mentioned, the Greeks stressed the importance of the speaker or arguer conveying *ethos* through what they said. In a case like the current one, it's the character of another person who is of interest. But it's an interesting, and I think relevant, feature of this case that Tom Udall was also on the list to be Interior secretary but he withdrew from consideration in order to support Haaland's candidacy. So, any force his argument may have is due to more than words, it's backed up with action. And so it may tell us something about the speaker's character as well.

18 Bad behavior (a failure of character)

Argument #18

> Having failed to make even a plausible case of widespread fraud or conspiracy before any court of law, the President has resorted to overt pressure on state and local officials to subvert the will of the people and overturn the election. It is difficult to imagine a worse, more undemocratic action by a sitting American President.
>
> Mitt Romney, November 19, 2020

We have seen people praising character, and the positive role that *ethos* can play in arguments. The other side to this is the criticism of character, criticism that can often undermine the acceptability of what a person argues, or at least diminish that person's credibility.

Following the US federal election in November 2020, there was a period of confusion and uncertainty during which the incumbent was disinclined to accept the results that saw his opponent win the presidency, and actively pursued means to retain the office for himself. Obviously, people differed in whether they thought this was an appropriate response. Republican Senator Mitt Romney was of no two minds about what was occurring, and this argument is part of his reaction. The argument above comes from his Twitter feed, but it was naturally picked up by multiple media outlets.

Given the relationships between character and actions that we have considered in the last two arguments, Romney's criticism of Trump's action here naturally reflects on his (Trump's) character. And of course, in the general background of relations between these two, especially during the impeachment process (see Argument #10), such a judgment is not surprising.

Attacks on character are ubiquitous in social argumentation, especially in the political sphere, and they are an important component of ethotic argument. The general term used for such attacks is *ad hominem* (an attack against the man, or person) and there are a number of varieties of this argument type. Readers are no doubt familiar with the term since it is one that has moved from the more rarified contexts of academic discussion into the public domain. Like some of the other argument types we have seen, it has traditionally been viewed as fallacious, since dismissing what someone says because of some feature of their character seems to be an irrelevant move. But, of course, we do allow that such arguments are reasonable if the circumstances are right. A witness who is shown to have committed perjury in the past cannot be trusted in what he or she says now. Indeed, they may well be telling the truth on this occasion, but the *ad hominem* dismissal will still have force. Likewise, if a political candidate has a history of failing to meet commitments, that inconsistency of character may well be exploited by an opponent. And those being asked to choose between the two candidates may well find the evidence of inconsistent commitments a character flaw that they cannot accept.

These two points show something of the range of the *ad hominem*. One case deals with what someone has said; the other with what they have done. But both reveal a problem with the person's character, and in such cases, character matters. So, *ad hominem* attacks are not always fallacious, and it falls to those of us considering such arguments to decide whether or not an attack is reasonable.

Douglas Walton, who we have met before, suggests that we are justified in being skeptical of arguments issued by people of bad character. But, of course, there need to be appropriate means for making that decision and so he offers some critical questions to help people consider individual cases. He requires that the allegation of bad character be supported by good evidence, for example (too many attacks simply devolve into verbal abuse). And he stresses the importance of determining that the issue of character is relevant to the case under question. Lastly, he allows that *ad homiem* arguments are often contributory to a judgment, but not decisive. That is, they will rarely stand alone. So, it is a matter of how strong a person's argument may be taken to be even after the issue of their bad character is decided. Should we, for example, assign only a reduced weight of credibility to the person and what they say rather than completely dismissing it, because the "total body of evidence available" in support of what they say warrants a more measured judgment? This is all good advice. We wouldn't want to dismiss a claim just because of who says it if there is other, independent support for that claim. Walton's questions help us to review Romney's argument.

Let's consider again what Romney is saying. He draws attention to two things that the President and his team had done: they had tried to have the results of the election overturned by various courts because of alleged widespread fraud or conspiracy. These attempts were unsuccessful, and Romney puts the lack of success down to the absence of any plausible argument. Second, the President had "resorted to overt pressure on state and local officials to subvert the will of the people and overturn the election." Neither of these charges amount to interpretations of what had been done, since the actions were a matter of public record. As reported in *The Hill* (the record of the case from which I am drawing), the President had reached out to various officials, like those in Wayne County, in order to have them block the certification of votes there (votes need to be certified before representative electors are sent to Washington for the vote of the electoral college). And the legal team, led by Rudy Giuliani, held a press conference in which they pursued claims of fraud "as part of an effort to sway the vote certification process and pressure state lawmakers to send pro-Trump electors to the Electoral College."

Two important claims are nestled within Romney's remarks: first, that no plausible arguments were given to show any widespread fraud, and second, that the actions described were attempts to "subvert the will of the people and overturn the election." From this, he concludes (and I think it is a concluding claim supported by the previous statements) that "It is difficult to imagine a worse, more undemocratic action by a sitting American President." Of this, the phrase, "It is difficult to imagine" is one that we can understand to mean, "I cannot imagine," or, simply and strongly: "no worse or more undemocratic action could be committed by a sitting American President." That last statement, especially as it is reworded here, is a powerful attack on the character of the President. But, as always, we reflect on whether it's a charitable recasting of what Romney says and accurately reflects what he believes. And it is: Romney accuses Trump of a bad character, witnessed (supported by) the bad (undemocratic) actions involved in an attempt to overturn the election results.

This is an *ad hominem* attack. It doesn't directly allege inconsistency of commitments. But I think it's reasonable to attribute to Romney the belief that a President of the United States is duty-bound to uphold the election results, and not doing so is thus inconsistent with the office he holds. Failure to uphold the integrity of the office is a failure of character. All of these are strong (and harsh) claims, but none is an unreasonable departure from Romney's statements.

Walton's suggested questions for evaluating the argument can now be applied, remembering that these are ways to access the contextual elements behind the statements rather than a definitive statement that something is good or bad.

First, is the allegation of bad character supported by good evidence? Here, we are led into the context and invited to ask on what grounds this is bad character on Trump's part. We need to consider the expectations that come with holding the office of president, and the role that office plays in upholding democracy. On the face of things, attempts to reverse the result of an election held on essentially the same terms as previous elections looks problematic. The evidence favors an affirmative response to this question.

Second, is the issue of character relevant to the case under question? Given the understanding of ethotic argumentation that the previous examples have provided us, we can see how an individual can reasonably judge character in light of actions. Given who it is who is being criticized, and the responsibilities that fall to him, then character does seem relevant here. These actions are not ones we would expect from a person who is trustworthy and committed to the best interests of the nation. Character is therefore relevant.

Finally, is the attack on character weakened by other, supplementary, evidence that supports the position of the person being attacked? This question takes us beyond the argument itself into the background situation and the events that were unfolding at the time. Charges of mass fraud were being repeated, along with fairly impassioned requests to report those charges. As the report in *The Hill* indicates (and this is representative of reports at the time), no corroborative support was given to the charges, at least not any that was sufficient to establish fraud at the level that would be necessary to steal an election. Romney would not have seen any supplementary evidence that should have given him pause and suggested he was not being fair. And, it can be noted, no such evidence was subsequently forthcoming.

On balance, this is a reasonable *ad hominem* argument. More importantly, it illustrates how such argumentation can be employed. On some occasions, concerns with someone's character do warrant a constructive argument bringing to light the flaws of that character. We just need practice at recognizing on which occasions this is a relevant strategy to pursue.

19 Damning character (the worse amongst us)

Argument #19

> Due to Vanier's almost legendary status, the abused women found it extremely difficult, if not impossible, to complain about his abuse. We see this ugly syndrome in churches in particular, because it's all the more dangerous when the culprit is considered especially holy or pious.
>
> Michael Coren, February 25, 2020

Jean Vanier is not exactly a household name, but his work is recognized the world over, a legacy that continues since his death in 2019. In the 1960s, he established the now-global community called L'Arche (named for Noah's Ark), a refuge for people with intellectual disabilities, where they could live and work together alongside people without such challenges. Religiously motivated, and operating within the parameters of the Catholic Church, the movement began when Mr. Vanier invited two mentally challenged men to live with him in a French village. By 2020, there were 154 such communities established in 30 countries.

Mr. Vanier had received the kind of praise that we saw bestowed on Justice Ginsburg in Argument #16. In 2015, Vanier received the Templeton Prize, an annual award made to a living person whose work harnesses the power of science to pose deep questions and explore humankind's place in the universe. The first recipient, in 1973, was Mother Teresa; a recent recipient in 2021 was Jane Goodall. Impressive company.

After his death, the L'Arche authorities conducted an internal study based on rumors of improprieties on Vanier's part. Made public in February 2020, the report corroborated six cases of sexual assault by Vanier on women associated with the organization. Although none of these women had disabilities, they had all struggled to gain a hearing in part because of the status of moral exemplar that Vanier enjoyed. This is the background to the *ad hominem* argument from Michael Coren, himself an Anglican priest. In structure and substance it is very different from Mitt Romney's attack on Donald Trump in Argument #18, but it is no less an ethotic argument, dealing with negative character. If some arguments praise character, others pinpoint flaws from which lessons can be drawn.

Coren is addressing a general audience in a daily newspaper, but his remarks may have particular resonance with the faith community. He sees the Vanier case as representative of what can occur in settings where individuals are surrounded by an aura of piety. So, his argument is as much against systemic issues endemic to a specific institution (like the church) that unheedingly provides the environment for abuse as it is against the individual abuser. Coren writes:

> We see this ugly syndrome in churches in particular, because it's all the more dangerous when the culprit is considered especially holy or pious.

The "because" is important, pointing to the supporting claim in a forceful way. His language, here and throughout his piece, is an unremitting part of his critique. "Grotesquely" and "repugnant" are joined here by "ugly syndrome" and "dangerous." There is emotion behind the words, and sometimes that can obscure the quality of the argument. But Coren's anger is reasonable, given what it is that has incited it and his own association with the religion he shares with Vanier. The ugly syndrome to which he refers is the difficulty abused women experience when trying to have their complaints heard and addressed. Vanier's "almost legendary status" would have exacerbated this experience for the women involved. And therein lies the principal issue with character. It can count for too much, or count where it should not. The praise for what Vanier accomplished was warranted, but not, we might say, the adoration that masked the reality of the man. After all, the examples of epideictic praise we have seen are naturally examples that involve exaggeration. A person is viewed selectively in terms of the good things that they have done and the corresponding positive values of character they possess. That's the focus of that type of ethotic argument. But there is always more to a person, and we can never lose sight of that. Ultimately, the positive values exemplified by a person can be detached from that character and promoted in themselves. Problems are not likely to arise when we praise people whose lives have ended, and this is why the memorial is such an effective vehicle for this type of argument. But when we praise living people, the situation is different. The aura of praise surrounding them, the pedestal on which they are put, can render them immune to the expectation that their moral behavior be like that of anyone else, and it can explain why others fail to see (or hear) the problem. If the structure of an institution like the church supports both the false immunity and the failure, then the criticism applies there as well. Coren covers both avenues. Perceptively, he notes elsewhere in the piece: "The truth about the pedestal is that those placed upon it do not make the climb on their own but are lifted by those around them." This, we have seen, is a result of ethotic argument, but it can also be its downside.

Coren's *ad hominem* is as strong as it is qualified. He certainly doesn't want to undermine the good things Vanier has done and what he has said. His target is a failure of character, and the failure of a person to live consistently with the principles he promotes through his faith. A critic might charge that with respect to his criticism of the church, Coren is generalizing from only one case. But this narrative is only one among many that have been detailed in the media, with the same moral and the same message, and it takes its place among them.

The Vanier case itself has further lessons about the relationship between *ethos* and value—the person and his or her actions. Chaim Perelman and Lucie Olbrechts-Tyteca, from whom I drew when discussing the case of Justice Ginsburg, have more to say about the subject: The "durable being" or "stable structure" that underlies a person's acts "permits us to prejudge" those acts. But the success in doing so depends very much on the accuracy of our information about the person in question. And this is where the import of the first critical question for exploring *ad hominem* arguments is again important: Is the allegation of bad character supported by good evidence?

This question would not have been raised in 2015, because there was no suggestion of Jean Vanier having a bad character. But if we replace "bad" with "good", we have a parallel question for exploring good ethotic appeals (and the other questions could be modified with the same substitution). So, we would have then asked: Is the allegation of *good* character supported by good evidence? In 2015, the answer to this was a confident affirmative. It is in the light of new evidence that the 2020 judgment about the person changes. This shift recommends against placing people on pedestals that are too lofty. But I don't think it undermines the argumentative strategy of using ethotic appeals to place the spotlight on community values and encouraging the adoption of those values and the appropriate dispositional attitudes that can follow. When we use argumentation in the service of values education, and when we deal with the complexities of social argumentation, we are always in the domain of uncertainty. But the rewards of adopting effective strategies outweigh the perils that can accompany them. As we struggle to find and adopt strategies that connect dispositions with values, we are most concerned with the public expression of those values. Other aspects of character may indeed be left in the private sphere of individual life. But in the end, we detach the value from the life as any epideictic speech ultimately aims to do. That is the force of representation. As I noted, Coren himself takes pains to separate his criticism of Vanier from the accomplishments of the L'Arche organization.

The life with the character it possesses is a conduit through which important values are conveyed, just as the centripetal force of argumentation aims to infuse those values into the characters of those who are learning. We get better at recognizing the right kinds of cases, and we get better at acting in the right kinds of ways. We become better disposed.

20 Associations (the company we keep)

Argument #20

> After four years of anti-establishment populism in power, its left-wing version no longer looks fresh or idealistic. What's more, revelations about Sander's history raise new questions about just how radical a candidate the self-proclaimed Democratic socialist is — as do some of his current associations … Sanders' nomination will be a disaster for America whether he wins or loses in November. There is still time for Democrats to come to their senses.
>
> Cathy Young, February 13, 2020

We are often judged according to the company we keep. Usually, this is unfortunate, and sometimes beside the point, but occasionally it is a relevant consideration. Again, in such cases, it's the "who" rather than the "what" that matters. Remember when your parents encouraged you to hang out with certain friends and keep away from others. They believed that the right kind of associations were good for you, just as the wrong kind were bad. That's what is behind the ethotic argument we are interested in here, the idea that it's the association rather than the action that is problematic and reflects badly on our character. If other people have some identifiable flaw, and we associate with them in some way, then the problem transfers to us and we are thought to have the same flaw or one that is similar.

The argument above is extracted from a much longer piece in *Newsday*, where columnist Cathy Young reviews Bernie Sanders' candidacy for the Democratic nomination for president. This is just after Sanders had won the New Hampshire Democratic primary and was considered the frontrunner and so projected to win the nomination. He also had had strong support before the 2016 election, losing out to Hillary Clinton, and during that campaign Young had defended Sanders against the claims of some of his detractors, one of which was that he was a communist. But in February 2020, she has changed her mind.

What is important for the extract of her reasoning that interests me is the associations she ascribes to Sanders. Videos of a trip to the Soviet Union in 1988—videos not available in 2016—raise concerns about his relationship with the Soviets. Young also refers to a statement of Sanders' praising Fidel Castro. This was from around the same time (1988) and found in the University of Vermont archives (Sanders was a senator from Vermont). She further singles out his association with the Marxist-Leninist Socialist Workers Party, writing:

> In 1980, Sanders was an elector for this fringe group at a time when it defended the Islamist revolution in Iran and its capture of the "imperialist" U.S. Embassy. He also spoke at rallies for its candidates in 1982 and 1984.

Finally, she adds that one of his chief campaign surrogates in 2020 "is militant anti-Israel activist Linda Sarsour," allegedly guilty of anti-Zionism rhetoric.

These associations, four in total, explain what Young is referring to in her argument by the revelations of Sanders' history and his current associations. And they thereby stand as the support for her conclusion that "Sanders' nomination will be a disaster for America, whether he wins or loses in November."

First, we can appreciate that this argument fits under the "ethotic" umbrella. Like those I have been considering in the previous few examples, it involves an attack on Sanders' character. But it differs from those examples because the strategy adopted is to criticize him for his associations, in the past and in 2020. Yes, like the criticisms of Trump by Romney and Vanier by Coren, there is a concern with his actions. But the actions in question arise via, and sometimes because of, the associations.

The particular type of ethotic argument that Young adopts has the traditional title of "Guilt by Association." Like the general *ad hominem*, this has usually been considered a fallacious move in argument: who one knows, it is asserted, should have no bearing on the acceptability of what one says. But also like the *ad hominem*, there are circumstances in which we are at least skeptical of what a person says if there are known associations that are likely to have influenced what was said, and those associations are problematic. Associations with gangs and racist groups always raise concerns, and these concerns seemed particularly pronounced during 2020. So, people were familiar with the type of reasoning we have here.

Young's argument, to be clear, is that Sander's nomination will be a disaster for America, whether or not he wins because of his past and present associations. So, to consider whether this attack on Sanders is reasonable, we need to consider both whether the associations existed or exist and, importantly, whether they are relevant in this case. After all, we can have all kinds of associations in certain areas of our lives that have no relation to what we say and do in other areas.

In fact, there are some specific questions we can ask here. I developed these with my co-author Leo Groarke in an earlier examination of Guilt by Association arguments. (We also recognized that honor or praise could be extended to a person because of who they associated with, but that's not at issue here). We consider a Guilt by Association argument to be strong if affirmative answers can be given to the following questions:

1 Is there good reason to believe that the alleged association between the person and another individual or group really does (or did) exist?
2 Is there good reason to question the beliefs or behavior of the "guilty" person or group? That is, can we corroborate the charge of "guilty!" in this case?
3 Is there no good reason to differentiate the person from the guilty individual or group?

As always, questions like these take us into the background of a case and allow us to explore it in its full context. Let's consider each point in turn in light of the information Young provides and any additional research that might be necessary.

For #1, we explore the claimed associations between Sanders and the USSR, Castro, the Marxist-Leninist Socialist Workers Party, and Linda Sarsour. Young cites her sources for two of the first three, although they all stem from the 1980s, and that may matter for the degree of weight we give them. The videos of Sanders' 1988 trip to the Soviet Union were discussed in a *Washington Post* article of May 3, 2019, and that article mentions the videos appearing on a Vermont community television station earlier in 2019. So, they are a matter of public record. In the videos, Sanders says what Young claims he said.

The praise of Fidel Castro is recorded in *The Washington Examiner*, where reference is made to the University of Vermont archives. Public record again. Sanders praises the revolution in Cuba for creating a different value system to that in the United States. No source is given for the association with the Marxist-Leninist Socialist Workers Party. But if he spoke at rallies for their candidates in 1982 and 1984, as she claims, then a record exists of this association as well.

However, as noted, these associations are all from the 1980s, three to four decades earlier. This may well matter to how strong we judge the support they provide for Young's conclusion. Because over time people tend to change the way they think and what they believe. Not day to day, it's to be hoped, but over several decades, yes. Young is concerned that Sanders has never publicly apologized for these associations, and that's a relevant concern for a public figure interested in amassing a public following. So, on balance, the support is weak but still relevant.

Linda Sarsour is a political activist, who co-chaired the 2017 Women's March. She is a controversial figure with a Palestinian background, outspoken in support of racial justice and civil rights. She is the kind of person, given his left-wing sympathies, with whom we are not surprised to see Sanders associating. And she did support his campaign. The association is there.

The second two considerations do not take as long to review as the first. We ask, for example, about the nature of the "guilt" that each of the associates allegedly has and transfer to Sanders. And I place the key word in scare quotes exactly because it can have a subjective quality to it. Not everyone would be concerned by the same things. Of course, there are some actions that concern everyone, like child abuse. There would be clear guilt in a case like that. But we don't have that here. Three of the associates are guilty of pursuing a leftist, perhaps non-American, political agenda. What might they transfer to Sanders? A desire for Marxist revolt? That would alarm most readers. A concern for issues of social justice? That would alarm fewer readers. We cannot give a definitive response to the "guilt," here because the matter needs to be viewed through the perspectives of different readers. Linda Sarsour, however, as a Palestinian-American, does espouse anti-Israel sentiments. And that would alarm an identifiable subset of readers. So, there is less doubt about her views, even though many Americans would share them or have sympathy for them.

Finally, we ask whether there are reasons to differentiate Sanders from his associates on things that matter. And we have seen that such reasons might lie in the dated associations involved with three of the four. These were not recent, nor were the views he expressed in the 1980s repeated in the same way. So, those associations, while real, are weaker than stronger. And with Linda Sarsour the case is even more difficult. The association is there, but could Sanders be differentiated on what matters, which is the anti-Israel remarks made by Sarsour? And he can. A December 2019 story in *The Times of Israel* notes that Sarsour backs Sanders, but not his support of Israel. So, on this issue (the one that Young identifies as problematic) they disagree. It's a relevant disagreement for our purposes.

So, on balance, we don't have the strongest "Guilt by Association" argument. Each of our three considerations provides cause to doubt the reasonableness of the argument. It might also be noted that Young's conclusion seems to overstep the evidence she provides. A Sanders' nomination, she says, will be a disaster for America, whether or not he wins in November. We might see, given the associations, that she could believe he would be a disaster if he wins, but why would this be the case if he loses? A review of her piece doesn't really answer this question, and the burden of proof lay with her to provide the support that would answer it. So, this remains a further weakness in an interesting but flawed argument.

21 The power of the expert (who you are and what you know matters)

Argument #21

> Travel restrictions and business closures aimed at stopping the spread of a new virus that has killed more than 300 people in China could end up causing ripple effects that harm the global economy, experts say. "When you stop planes and ships, trains and motor vehicles from moving, it starts to shut down the economy -- and that can have a cascading effect throughout society," Dr. Eric Toner, senior scholar at the Johns Hopkins Center for Health Security... "And it's not just airline pilots who get out of work, I mean, it's you know, it's everybody that they depend on."
>
> CTV News report, Feb 1, 2020

On balance, the year 2020 was not a good year for experts. People began to express doubts about some expert claims when disagreements between them emerged, or when an expert source changed their mind in a short period of time. As I have noted in earlier examples, we rely on expert testimony in so many areas of our lives where we simply do not have the knowledge to assess a claim, or the time to develop such knowledge. But when experts seem to fail, the trust in the type of argument that relies on expert knowledge is diminished.

The argument above relies on expert opinion, so it will give us an opportunity to consider the force such arguments have and when they are reasonable. The expert in question is Dr. Eric Toner, and the news media source is appealing to him for reasons why travel restrictions and business closures during the pandemic could be a bad thing. Again, note that this is early in the year 2020, when people did not know what was to come or what actions would be best for responding to the spread of the virus. Experts were a natural and necessary source to turn to for information.

The claim is that "travel restrictions and business closures aimed at stopping the spread of a new virus could end up causing ripple effects that harm the global economy." The reasons supporting this claim (and, presumably, the claim itself) come from Dr. Toner. He believes:

- Premise 1: When you stop planes and ships, trains and motor vehicles from moving, it starts to shut down the economy -- and that can have a cascading effect throughout society.
- Premise 2: And it's not just airline pilots who get out of work; it's everybody that they depend on.

Two reasons, then, to think that travel restrictions will have an impact on the economy. But why should we accept Dr. Toner's word? As I said, the pandemic put a serious strain on the way members of society processed and accepted expert testimony. There were reasons for that, and I'll consider them shortly. But first let's consider the nature of appeals to expert testimony and how to judge them.

There are clear criteria by which we judge appeals to expert arguments, and they focus on the nature of the expert. In the first instance, we need to have identifiable experts with clear credentials. This is because we need to be able to verify that they are experts, and in principle be able to do our own research into them. In most cases, we won't be looking up the background of alleged experts, but it must be possible for us to do so should we choose to do it. You have seen reports where it is claimed "experts believe," and then some claim is asserted. But this is unhelpful, particularly at a time when people seem to believe just about anything. We need to know who those experts are and what credentials they have that make them experts. Second, they need to be the right kind of experts for the area of concern, or the claim made. Having an expert in one field offering a claim about something in a different field is again unhelpful, since the expert may have no better knowledge of the other field than anyone else.

In the argument we are considering, the expert is identified, along with something of his credentials. Dr. Toner is a senior scholar at the Johns Hopkins Center for Health Security. That's enough information for us to look up Dr. Toner and his research center and make a judgment about how a strong an expert he is. The Johns Hopkins Center for Health Security is an established research center with a relevant history. It began operating in 1998 as the first non-governmental organization to study the vulnerability of US civilian populations to biological weapons and how to prevent, prepare, and respond to their consequences. This is relevant to the concerns of the current pandemic. Dr. Toner is a recognized scholar at the center with a particular expertise in internal and emergency medicine. Here, though, it is more difficult to see the relevant connection. The issue involves the relationship between transportation and economics. If we were asked who a relevant expert would be to discuss such an issue, we would likely suggest an economist or someone whose research was transportation, and preferably a person who crossed these fields. It's not clear that an expert in internal and emergency medicine is a relevant source here. And that's a serious problem with this argument.

Further conditions for assessing expert appeals include a check that the person is not biased in an inappropriate way. That is, for example, they do not stand to gain in any way if their expertise is accepted (other than the normal increase in status). This would not seem an issue in our argument.

Finally, sets of criteria for this type of argument often prefer to see consensus between experts in a field. This is a difficult criterion in many cases and may account for why people become skeptical of expert advice in many fields. On some questions, yes, we would expect any knowledgeable person in a field to have the same response. But on the kinds of questions about which we are likely to see argumentation, questions that involve issues of uncertainty, then a desire for consensus is unlikely to be fulfilled and may, in fact, mislead us. We know that important legal cases can involve experts testifying on both sides, for the defense and the prosecution. There, judges and juries have to weigh the plausibility of conflicting advice as best they can to decide which testimony is more reliable. And then there are cases, like the one we are discussing, where the relative novelty of the circumstances reduces the expectation that experts would agree. Of course, there have been viruses before that have had a global impact, but the economic realities would have been different then, as would the means and nature of transportation.

We emerge for this discussion with four criteria for assessing expert testimony, two of which do not seem relevant to the current argument, and one of which undermines it.

i   There is an identified expert source with clear credentials.
ii   The expert's claim/argument is in a field in which their expertise is relevant.
iii There is no obvious illegitimate bias on the part of the expert.
iv   And there is no expectation of consensus in the area of the argument.

What Dr. Toner says, does have plausibility. When you shut down transportation, that is likely to have a negative impact on the economy, including rates of employment. And that may well be a serious consideration that would lead some people to oppose travel restrictions and business closures, understanding that such a consideration would need to be weighed against health concerns (again, at a time when reliable information on the virus was in short supply). But the point for us is that, *as an 'appeal to expert testimony' argument*, since this is the principal strategy employed, the argument is weak. Criterion (ii) is not fulfilled, we do not have an expert speaking in the relevant area of his expertise.

As I noted at the outset, we are very reliant on experts for so much of the information we have and on which we act (consider how readily you follow the advice of your doctor, for example, and then trust the medications you are prescribed). This is unavoidable. It is simply not practical for us to try and verify all the claims that are out there and for which we don't have the right education or training. But some claims are more easily accepted on expert testimony than others, just as some experts are more easily trusted. During the pandemic there was a decrease in such trust, due in part to the lack of consensus on many questions and the revising of information by the same expert on different occasions.

There are several reasons for the poor performance of experts in this case. For the most part, and particularly in the early part of 2020, there simply was no clear "knowledge" that experts could use and communicate. A new virus operating in novel circumstances encouraged speculation and guesswork but not knowledge claims. Yet, society still turned to "experts" for advice and demanded they say something. This put many otherwise knowledgeable people in an untenable situation, forced to talk about something that was generally unclear, commenting on the impartial results of

The power of the expert (who you are and what you know matters)

uncorroborated studies, and changing their opinions as the data was increased. It is not surprising that they failed in the ways they did. Moreover, they were often forced into news events where they became public speakers without the training needed to communicate in that way. The resulting hesitancy and the sometimes contradictory statements did nothing to improve the flagging image of expertise in our society.

Under normal circumstances, however, and once the evidence has been amassed to support knowledgeable communications, the appeal to an expert is a valuable type of argument. You can expect to see and use many more of them.

Part IV
Strategies of reason

22 Using threats (let this be a warning)

Argument #22

> Let this serve as a WARNING that if Iran strikes any Americans, or American assets, we have…targeted 52 Iranian sites (representing the 52 American hostages taken by Iran many years ago), some at a very high level & important to Iran & the Iranian culture, and those targets, and Iran itself, WILL BE HIT VERY FAST AND VERY HARD. The USA wants no more threats!
>
> NBC News, January 4, 2020

Is it ever reasonable to use threats to achieve an end? On the face of things, it would appear not. We promote reasonable discourse and thoughtful engagement whenever possible. But then, on the other hand, there are labor negotiations where one side threatens to withdraw services, and another to lock out its workers. The usual conditions for avoiding such actions include bargaining in "good faith." Or, a convicted person is warned that should they reoffend, the next penalty they are given will not be so lenient. Or, a country bristles or wilts in the face of threatened sanctions if it does not act in a specific way dictated by the threatening nation or a coalition of nations. In each of these common and recognizable cases, reasonable discourse seems to be bypassed or replaced by a clear threat. In some circumstances, then, the use of threats is a natural part of the processes involved, and no one is surprised by them.

To refer to this as an argument—something we have seen at the core of reasoned discourse—seems at first to be a contradiction. But we have a claim in terms of a specific action that is being advised or promoted and reasons given with the intention of bringing about that action. The appeal to threats is a recognized type of argument and, as one might imagine, it has a history as long as human conflict itself.

As with several types of argument I have explored in this book, this one has usually been represented as fallacious, for the reasons that were suggested in the previous paragraphs. It often goes by a Latin name, *Argumentum ad Baculum*, which means an "argument that appeals to the stick." English philosopher John Locke (1632–1704) is credited with introducing a class of ad-fallacies into the language, and later philosopher Jeremy Bentham (1748–1832) included an appeal to fear or threats in his *Handbook of Political Fallacies* (1824). It is sometimes called an appeal to fear because, presumably, the threat invokes fear in the intended recipient.

But also for the reasons I have already noted, not every instance of the appeal to threat (let's stay with the English name) is obviously fallacious. So, as before, we need to consider conditions under which it should—and should not—be acceptable. Let's first look more carefully at the argument we have.

Qasem Soleimani, one of Iran's top generals was assassinated on January 3rd by a drone strike at Baghdad International Airport. The United States took responsibility for the attack, saying they had acted to prevent Soleimani planning and executing attacks on coalition bases in Iraq. In the heightened tensions that immediately followed between the two nations, the expectation that Iran would find some way to retaliate was natural. The argument, contained in one of President Trump's tweets, was a proactive effort to prevent such retaliation.

The conclusion is clear, if implicit: Iran should not strike any Americans or American assets. The reason given for why they should not is that doing so would result in immediate strikes on 52 Iranian sites, some of cultural value. There is a further hidden premise here to the effect that Iran will not want to have (or would fear having) these 52 sites attacked. In these terms, it is a classic *ad baculum*. The threat is clear, the attempt to invoke fear is there, and there's a clear indication of what to do (or avoid doing) in order to respond to the threat.

These last points indicate the kinds of questions we should be asking here. Earlier in the book, I drew attention to the role of argumentation schemes in the theory and study of arguments. This last section of the book explores different strategies that are expressed through argumentation schemes, with the appeal to threat being the first. As a scheme, we expect a set of questions that allow us to explore the thick context behind the thin description given in the argument pattern.

The first such question asks whether the person (or group) issuing the threat is in a position to bring about the threatened action. People routinely make threats but do not always have the resources or authority to carry through with them. That's not the case here. In fact, a further tweet from Trump, a day later, compounds the threat in a way that directly answers this question:

> The United States just spent Two Trillion Dollars on Military Equipment. We are the biggest and by far the BEST in the World! If Iran attacks an American Base, or any American, we will be sending some of that brand new beautiful equipment their way...and without hesitation!

And, of course, he does have the authority to carry through on the threat, even though some congressional leaders raised concerns.

A second question asks whether the threat could be avoided in the way proposed, or whether the threatened action would occur anyway. Will the consequence occur regardless of the threat? That is, what is being threatened is already likely to happen. I think we can safely say that's not the case here. There's nothing to suggest those 52 Iranian sites are in any danger outside of the action threatened by Donald Trump.

Third, another question asks whether there's a way for the threatened party to avoid the threat. That is, are there clear ways to act so as to avoid the threatened action? This condition is met here. The United States is demanding that Iran not retaliate for the Soleimani killing. Such inaction would be sufficient to remove the threat.

Lastly, but importantly, is the threatened action proportional to what it is trying to promote or prevent? Some readers might have noticed an element of "just war" reasoning in this scheme. In his *Summa Theologica*, St. Thomas Aquinas discusses two famous doctrines, one of "double effect" and another of "proportionality" that suggest it may be permissible to respond to an action (like war) or an expected action (like an attack) if (i) someone is acting with the aim of preventing an identifiable wrong and (ii) the wrong which is committed is not out of proportion (and unduly wrong) when it is compared to the wrong which is prevented. This would place the argument we are considering (and others of the scheme) into a rich but controversial tradition, which includes justifications of self-defense.

This is where the primary weakness of Trump's argument becomes apparent—in its disproportionality. Yes, the argument fits the scheme and meets several of the criteria that govern such arguments. But the nature of what is threatened would seem to be quite disproportional to the admittedly vague retaliation that it tries to prevent. The threat involves attacking 52 sites (a number chosen because it corresponds to the number of US hostages held in the embassy in Tehran during Jimmy Carter's presidency in 1979). And, problematically, those sites include a number that have cultural significance. This aspect of the threat is stressed: "some [sites] at a very high level & important to Iran & the Iranian culture." It is difficult to imagine that the threatened action is proportional to what it aims to prevent, even given the vagueness of the latter. Moreover, as several commentators were quick to point out, attacking sites of cultural significance is a war crime under the 2017 resolution of the United Nations Security Council (Resolution 2347), which prohibits the targeting of cultural heritage sites. On this criterion, then, we have a weak argument.

The dark side of diplomacy will continue to see arguments of this nature, just as they will occur in other walks of life in which they are relevant. As we have seen, they require careful review to determine if and when they are fallacious. This situation received a lot of media attention at the start of January 2020, as might be expected. But very soon, the world's attention was directed elsewhere and to a threat of a very different nature.

23 Establishing precedents (what we do now matters later)

Argument #23

> [to cancel the Olympics] "would leave a very bad precedent for the Olympic Committee so the next city and the city after that would be aware of this risk, which might deter cities from bidding to host future Games"
>
> Takuji Okubo (North Asia Director, Economist Corporate Network), March 18, 2020

Do you remember the Tokyo Olympics held in the summer of 2020? No, no one does. They didn't happen as planned, another casualty of the pandemic sweeping the world. The 2020 Summer Olympics took place in Tokyo from July 23 to August 8, *2021*, a year later than scheduled. But that non-happening was despite the very best efforts of many people, in deeds and in argument.

There are a number of strategies that might be employed by someone advocating for the Games to go ahead. The one chosen by Takuji Okubo is to argue that cancelling the Games, as several people were proposing in March of 2020, would set a bad precedent with a result that nobody really wants. Let's see how the reasoning in the argument works:

- Premise 1: If the Tokyo Olympic Games are cancelled, this would establish a precedent for cancelling future games.
- Premise 2: The next city to act as hosts would then be aware there is a risk of cancellation, as would the city after that, and so forth.
- Sub-Conclusion: Cities might be deterred from bidding to host future Games.
- Hidden Sub-conclusion: This would be an undesirable outcome for the Olympic Committee.

DOI: 10.4324/9781003326328-28

108   *Strategies of reason*

- Hidden Main Claim: The Tokyo Olympic Games should not be cancelled.

You can see I have extrapolated a lot from what Mr. Okubo says as I reconstruct and standardize his reasoning to fit the scheme that I believe he is employing. But, as before, the test is to stand back and ask whether he is committed to the statements I have attributed to him. And, further, whether he is using this strategy that we call "Appeal to Precedent." Obviously, I believe he is. He is raising a concern for his audience (the Olympic Committee) by indicating an outcome that they should find undesirable. And the way to avoid the outcome is not to cancel the Games, a conclusion to which Mr. Okubo is obviously committed.

In identifying this as an Appeal to Precedent, I class it as analogical reasoning. That is, the force of the argument, as with any precedent, depends on future cases being analogous to the current case. It is then the comparison between cases and their circumstances that matters. I say this because some people might judge this to be a different argumentation scheme to which is bears remarkable similarities: that is the future-looking causal scheme called a "Slippery Slope."

In Slippery Slope reasoning, the reason for not doing a proposed action (or doing it, if the outcome is positive) is that it would set off a causal chain leading to an undesirable outcome. To avoid that outcome, we don't take the first step in the chain and avoid doing the proposed action. For example:

> If the minimum wage for restaurant and bar workers is raised, this will put more financial strain on business owners already struggling from the effects of the pandemic, they will then either layoff some of their staff or decrease their hours. This will result in financial hardships for the very group that the pay raise was supposed to help (an undesirable outcome), So, the minimum wage for restaurant and bar workers should not be raised.

Perhaps there's a sense of a precedent being set by raising the minimum wage, but that's not really what is going on here. The concern is that a policy or action will set off a causal chain of reactions, hence the slipperiness of a slope that once we start down we cannot prevent. The reasoning strategy is causal, not analogical. The quality of the argument depends on whether the one step in the chain will lead, causally, to the next, and so forth. The quality of an Appeal to Precedent depends upon the similarities and dissimilarities between cases.

Underlying the Appeal to Precedent, then, is a hidden assumption that operates as a guiding principle: *Doing x will establish a precedent whereby all similar cases should be treated the same.* In our case, x = cancelling the Tokyo Olympics. Treating similar cases the same is the idea behind appealing to precedents in legal proceedings, which is one of the principal places we are likely to find them.

Identified this way, the argument we have is a variant of the Argument from Analogy. I will focus on this in Argument #28. With such arguments the number of similarities between cases and the absence of serious dissimilarities will help us recognize when we have strong examples. We can anticipate some of that discussion here in considering whether the cases imagined by Takuji Okubo would be similar and, importantly, would not be dissimilar. Those are two of the main questions to ask in establishing *whether* a precedent would indeed be set by a cancellation. Because if it would not, then this argument against cancelling the Games is weak.

A further question to pose for Appeal to Precedent arguments is whether the alleged outcome, in this case having cities deterred from bidding to host future Games, would indeed be undesirable. Here, it clearly would, given that the audience for Okubo's argument is the Olympic Committee and those who might influence its members. Of course, there are always groups that oppose their cities making bids to host the Games, usually for economic reasons. They would be delighted by such an outcome. But they are not the audience for this argument. The Olympic Committee should be concerned by any precedent that would reduce bids and generally undermine the "Olympic brand." So, this question is answered in the affirmative: the precedent would lead to an undesirable outcome. Or, we should say, could lead to it, because, in fairness to Mr. Okubo, he has qualified his claim: the risk *might deter* future cities from bidding. He has recognized the uncertainty of any outcome when we argue this way about future events. Still, he raises an important concern that his audience would take seriously.

But how worried should the Olympic Committee be? To decide this, we ask about similarities and dissimilarities. It is difficult to decide on how similar future bidding cities would be because they are not identifiable at this stage. Usually with analogical reasoning, we have identified cases being compared, and so we can consider just how similar they are. But it's reasonable to expect that the

Olympic Committee would use the same criteria when considering future bids as they have done in the past. And so, only cities that meet the conditions required (having sufficient sites, financial commitments, and so forth) would qualify as potential bidders. So, we are anticipating similar cases.

When we turn to dissimilarities, however, we look specifically at the reasons behind the precedent. What is it about the Tokyo Games that makes them susceptible to cancellation? And here, we might imagine we have a circumstance that is not likely to be easily replicated. What threatened the Tokyo Summer Olympics in March 2020 was a global pandemic. It did eventually lead to a year's postponement (which itself would now be considered a precedent). But unless we imagine that events of such magnitude could become more regular, the situation that would lead to a cancellation has to be considered a rare event that would not be seen as a risk for future bidders. At least, this is likely to make a difference in the deliberations of the Olympic Committee. Yes, future cities may well be deterred from bidding during times of global pandemics. And it was the case that the pandemic influenced global events for several years. But the Summer Olympics happen once every four years, so that's a sufficient gap for any pandemic to play out. Plus, what is learned from one such global pandemic may decrease the risk of other similar pandemics from occurring and interfering in major events. These are the kinds of considerations that would play out in the Olympic Committee's deliberations. So, the Committee can be confident that cancelling these Games would not set a precedent that is likely to recur or encourage other cities to worry about the risk of it doing so. Mr. Okubo's argument has a serious weakness.

We do set precedents when we act, sometimes we deliberate over them. And, we use arguments to support doing so as well as warning against the risks involved. Like other future-looking arguments, they lack guarantees. But they raise important considerations that encourage us to move carefully when we act for change or when we anticipate the future. And they show us something about how important analogical arguments are in our daily reasoning. We will see more of this.

24 A causal chain (if this, then that)

Argument #24

> Ceasing all export of respirators produced in the United States would likely cause other countries to retaliate and do the same, as some have already done. If that were to occur, the net number of respirators being made available to the United States would actually decrease. That is the opposite of what we and the Administration, on behalf of the American people, both seek.
>
> 3M April 3, 2020

3M Company is an important, even critical, supplier of respirator masks. This fact came to the fore in April 2020 after President Trump halted exports of the masks to Canada and Latin America under the Defense Production Act. Now, there might have been moral arguments against doing so, and 3M did also cite "significant humanitarian implications" of not providing respirator masks. But that wasn't the principal choice of strategy adopted by the company. They provide a future-looking causal argument of the kind I used in the last entry (Argument #23) to distinguish such reasoning from Appeals to Precedent. They are bringing to light possible consequences of the policy that may not have been anticipated, arguing that an action taken in support of American interests may actually be counterproductive for those interests.

In this argument, there is no underlying strategy of analogical reasoning. The company anticipates other countries doing the same thing, but that's as far as comparison enters the discourse. Instead, it's causal connections that they stress. There are two of them, resulting in an undesirable outcome.

- Premise 1: Ceasing all export of respirators produced in the United States would likely cause other countries to retaliate and do the same, as some have already done.

- Premise 2: If that were to occur (i.e., retaliation), the net number of respirators being made available to the United States would actually decrease.
- Premise 3: [A decreased supply to the US] is the opposite of what we and the Administration, on behalf of the American people, both seek [This is an undesirable result].
- Hidden Conclusion: The White House should rescind its order to cease all export of respirators produced in the United States.

So, the argument fits the Slippery Slope scheme that was seen in Argument #23, illustrating further the difference between analogical and causal reasoning. This is the place to think more carefully about the Slippery Slope. Like the *ad hominem*, Slippery Slope has become a part of the everyday vernacular. This indicates the prevalence of the argument pattern, one that we are often likely to encounter. And even if they are not sure exactly what is involved, most people are likely to associate Slippery Slope arguments with bad ones.

Indeed, it regularly appears on lists of fallacies, although it's less obvious why this is the case. I've seen some pretty fuzzy explanations of what's wrong with it. Maybe it fails to engage in the issue at hand (a problem of irrelevance), or there is little or no evidence provided for the causal chain. These would both be concerns, but there's nothing about the scheme that includes these flaws as characteristics of the reasoning. Let me suggest three questions that any example of the scheme must satisfy in order to be judged reasonable. Failure to offer a satisfactory answer to any of the questions indicates a weak argument, and likely a fallacious one.

1 Is each of the causal steps plausible?
2 Could one stop at any stage and not proceed further, or is the slope indeed "slippery"?
3 Is the alleged outcome really negative?

For previous schemes, the crucial question has tended to be the last; here it's the first, because this question explores the causal links on which the argument depends for any force that it has. Those who believe that the scheme involves arguments where little or no evidence is provided for the causal chain have been exposed to examples where the causal links are unsupported. But, in principle, that need not be the case. We have two causal claims in the first two premises of this argument: (i) Ceasing all export of respirators produced in the United States *would likely cause* other countries to retaliate and do the same; and (ii) retaliation by other countries would cause the net number of respirators being made available to the United States to actually decrease.

> For the first of these claims, I have put some words in italics to show that we, again, have a qualified claim. 3M is not saying that stopping exports *will* cause retaliation, but that it might. That's fair. This is not the kind of causal relationship where we see a constant connection between two things operating under normal conditions (throw the light switch, and the light comes on). The main concern, though, is whether the causal link is plausible. The last clause suggests it is. We read "as some have already done." Of course, there's slight ambiguity here. Countries may have restricted exports to the United States already (without any prompting from the United States), or, they may have started to do it in retaliation. In the context, we read it as the second (it's still relevant, but weaker, if the first meaning is correct). This would then need to be verified as a matter of public record, requiring us to look further into the background.

Canadian Prime Minister Justine Trudeau, while stopping short of imposing retaliatory measures, stressed the enormous amount of trade in essential services that goes back and forth between Canada and the United States. But evidence of actual retaliation is not readily available (and wasn't at the time), and the onus was on 3M to provide evidence in support of that claim.

The second causal connection is between retaliation by other countries and a net decrease in respirators being available to the United States. This is a crucial claim, since it links with the information in Premise 3, that the United States move will be counterproductive. The claim implies that the United States depends not just on domestic production of respirators but also foreign suppliers. Looking into the background of the issue, it becomes clear that 3M produces many of its products in other countries, and the exporting of what it produces elsewhere could be blocked by the host countries. This is indicated in some of the additional comments in the lead story. The White House had allegedly pressured 3M to "export 10 million N95 masks from its Singapore facilities rather than sending them to its markets in Asia." And the company also explained that it had just "secured approval from China" to export millions of masks that it had manufactured there to the United States. These background facts render the causal relationship more plausible, since it is quite possible that the number of masks 3M is prevented from bringing into the United States exceeds the number that it is blocked from exporting to Canada and Latin America. It is a stronger premise than the first because of this.

The second question essentially asks whether the final step is inevitable once the causal chain is set in process. That's the sense of slipperiness that the scheme involves. This will separate the scheme from other arguments that simply predict a causal outcome. It matters that there is more than one causal step, and that the second follows directly from the first, and so forth. The causal claim in the second premise is stronger than the qualified claim in the first. It tells us that if there is retaliation, the net amount of masks available to Americans *would* decrease. The company must know that more masks are produced internationally than domestically. So, if the retaliation occurs and is of the same nature (that is, no exporting of masks), then the claimed effect will occur. Charitably, we should read it this way unless or until we have information to suggest it is wrong. So, I am prepared to allow that, once started, the causal connections are strong. It's just a question of whether it will start.

In a similar fashion, the last question is quickly addressed. It is accurate in this case: the outcome would be counterproductive if fewer masks are available as a result of a policy that was intended to ensure a supply of masks for Americans.

On balance, there's enough strength in the argument to warrant reflection on the part of the intended audience (the White House). They will need to gauge the risk of retaliation, since that's the main issue that the information we have leaves unclear.

To reiterate, we have a quite different strategy than we saw with the previous argument, despite the similarity of the patterns, and we see argument being used in different ways to fit a circumstance and respond to an urgent situation.

25 Negative consequences (if this, then also that)

Argument #25

> If we skip over the checkpoints in the guidelines to 'Open America Again,' then we risk the danger of multiple outbreaks throughout the country. This will not only result in needless suffering and death, but would actually set us back on our quest to return to normal.
>
> Dr. Anthony Fauci, May 11, 2020

In the forward-looking causal argument of #24, I indicated that not all such reasoning would involve a slope and a series of causal links. Some arguments look simply at the negative outcome of an action as a means to persuade people to respond in specific ways. This is the strategy we see Dr. Anthony Fauci adopting in this example. In particular, he is employing what we call an Argument from Negative Consequences. This is a variant of the general Argument from Consequences scheme, which promotes or demotes something in light of the consequences it is predicted to have.

Consequentialist reasoning is notoriously difficult, particularly in the ethical domain. In some of the discussions of character is the previous part of the book, thinking in terms of consequences was contrasted with thinking involved in virtue ethics. As we saw, while aspects of character are private and hidden from view, consequences are public and available for inspection. But that is only after they have occurred. We can well judge the correctness of something after the consequences are available. But when it is a matter of predicting what consequences will follow, different considerations are involved.

When we appeal to the consequences of an action or policy, no matter whether we judge them negative or positive, we are expected to give some indication of how likely it is that the alleged consequences will occur. We may also need to review the extent of the sphere in which the consequences will fall and the number of people affected. This is a consideration for the utilitarian, for example, who is concerned to see the promotion of greatest number of preferences for the greatest number of people involved in or affected by the action. But who is involved? How large is the sphere of influence for any of our actions? A stone thrown into the lake creates a ripple effect that diminishes as the circumference expands. Something similar occurs in the realm of action. And the thinker who deals in consequences must weigh the negative against the positive. We often see negative outcomes to what is proposed, but judge that they are counteracted by more likely positive outcomes. Or, the nature of the negative consequences is just not judged severe enough to make a difference one way or the other.

With these complications in mind, let's turn to the scheme that Fauci is using, the Argument from Negative Consequences. The thin pattern that expresses the scheme is straightforward:

- Premise: If an action/policy, A, is brought about then B will/may occur.
- Premise: B is a negative outcome.
- Conclusion: Therefore, A should not be brought about.

Were we arguing in favor of adopting an action or policy, we would identify a positive outcome in the second premise. But Dr. Fauci is arguing a negative case. During a period (May 2020) when the pandemic has necessitated the closing of many businesses and necessitated restrictions on trade, he is concerned about the risk of opening the economy too quickly. His audience is the Health Education, Labor and Pensions Committee of the US Senate, the decision-making body in question. After identifying the principal strategy of argument used by an arguer, I have often had to make adjustments when fitting it into the pattern of the scheme. But this one fits without question.

- Premise: If America is reopened too early (we skip over the checkpoints in the guidelines to 'Open America Again'), then we risk the danger of multiple outbreaks throughout the country, resulting in needless suffering and death and actually setting back our quest to return to normal.
- Premise: Needless suffering and death and being set back in our quest to return to normal is a negative outcome.

– Conclusion: Therefore, America should not be opened too early.

From what I suggested above, we can devise three critical questions (CQs) to help us explore the thick description of the case, delving further into the context that supports it.

– CQ1: How strong is the likelihood that the cited consequences will (may) occur?
– CQ2: How great is the impact or extent of the likely consequences, and is it sufficient to support the strength of the conclusion?
– CQ3: Are there other opposite consequences (good as opposed to bad, for example) that should be taken into account?

These questions pose important considerations for people weighing the merits of an action or policy. We know that our actions have consequences, but will they necessarily be negative, and might they be offset by other, more positive ones? The first critical question here is crucial, because we respond differently to negative outcomes that must occur than to those that might. Fauci is not as clear as he might be. Opening too soon poses a *risk* of danger, and this *will* result in needless suffering, deaths, and so forth. So, how high is the risk? And, more specifically, what constitutes opening too soon, because the risks are surely tied to this? The White House distributed a 20-page document with guidelines: "Opening Up America Again." This serves as our guide in considering the previous questions. Before a state or region moves to phased openings there must be, for example, a downward trajectory of symptomatic cases in the previous 14 days, and a downward trajectory of documented cases and positive tests, and also the absence of crisis care for patient treatment along with a robust testing program for health care workers. Taken together, that's a rigorous set of conditions that need to be met. Opening up too soon would mean opening before all or some of those conditions are met (people might debate how many are relevant). In light of this understanding of what it would mean to open too soon, the sense of risk gains a more concrete meaning. Together with the further conviction on Fauci's part of what will result, we can be satisfied that there is a strong likelihood of what he proposes occurring.

In similar terms, we can gauge the "ripple effect" involved in this consequences argument. The White House document refers to states or regions, so the reopening is envisaged on a regional basis according to local data. Given the varying strains on health care resources in different regions, the impact could be greater in some than in others. But it is reasonable to judge the impact will be significant in any locality.

The last question, in the context of this issue, is likely to match health care outcomes against economic outcomes, assuming that it is the latter that is behind any push to open early. The audience for the argument—the Senate Committee on Health Education, Labor and Pensions—has broad jurisdiction over US health care, education, employment, and retirement policies, so its concerns will cover both health consequences and those that have an economic bearing. The focus of the White House document on reopening, however, has a distinct stress on health issues because, after all, that is what has motivated the closing to begin with. Earlier reopening could have initial positive consequences for the economy. But would they last? It's a feature of Fauci's argument that he believes they would not, that early reopening would ultimately be a set back to what had already been achieved. So, the last question is implicitly addressed, and positively so.

On balance, Fauci's argument is reasonable, and it helps us to see how we should handle arguments of this kind. They project us into an unknown future and ask us to imagine what it will be like. The lesson is not to detach that imagination from what we know about the patterns of reasonable consequences arguments.

26 An unexpected outcome (the benefit of a pandemic)

Argument #26

> One of the paradoxical consequences of the global crisis triggered by the COVID-19 is its impact on the environment. The quarantine is causing sharp declines in pollutant emissions across the world's most populated cities...In Spain, according to a report by Greenpeace, traffic in Madrid and Barcelona, the two largest cities in the country, dropped by 60% during the first days of the state of alarm, resulting in a sharp decline in pollution levels. Vehicles are the main source of emissions in Spain. Thus, median NO2 levels, caused mainly by diesel engine activity, dropped below the 40 percent limit established by the World Health Organization (WHO) and the European Union (EU) as safe for humans.
>
> BBVA, a global financial services group, March 25, 2020

Sometimes, a causal argument points to something positive. And in this example, we witness the indirect positive effects of a pandemic. People are encouraged or required to self-isolate, and that forces changes in behavior. One of those forced changes is less movement, locally and internationally. Airlines drastically reduce their operations, and cars and buses disappear from the roads as most people work from home.

Any argument that claims to identify the cause of a phenomenon is complex, but this argument is complex in other ways. Beyond the causal argument in which I am interested, there is an appeal to expert opinion (Greenpeace), and inductive generalization (making a claim about the world's most populated cities based on evidence from two cities in one country), and an implicit argument from analogy (what is the case in Spain will be the case elsewhere). Either of the last two schemes could be used to evaluate the reasoning if

DOI: 10.4324/9781003326328-31

they were taken to be the principal strategy of argument employed. But, influenced in part by the title of the piece BBVA released, I take the principal strategy to be causal and will approach the argument as involving a causal claim. This claim, at least, is clear: the drop in emissions brought on by the pandemic quarantine caused a drop in pollution emissions across the world. In this way, the pandemic due to COVID-19 had a positive aspect to it. During a year in which environmental concerns were also receiving a lot of media attention, this was a relevant issue.

Perhaps it is more charitable to restrict the argument to the information about Spain. That's where the causal evidence lies. The extrapolation from the two Spanish cities to the rest of the world is unsupported and is a weakness in the overall reasoning. We still need to be satisfied that Madrid and Barcelona are representatives of "major" Spanish cities, but that's a much easier claim to admit. Using only part of the information, then, the argument is the following:

- Premise 1: In Spain, [according to a report by Greenpeace], traffic in Madrid and Barcelona, the two largest cities in the country, dropped by 60% during the first days of the state of alarm, resulting in a sharp decline in pollution levels.
- Premise 2: Vehicles are the main source of emissions in Spain.
- Sub-conclusion: median NO2 levels, caused mainly by diesel engine activity, dropped below the 40 percent limit established by the World Health Organization (WHO) and the European Union (EU) as safe for humans.
- Main Conclusion: One of the paradoxical consequences of the global crisis triggered by the COVID-19 is its impact on the environment.

I have added the main conclusion from the start of the piece because it is supported by the case from Spain. I could have stopped with the sub-conclusion. It was introduced by a conclusion word "thus," and the scheme involved is a causal scheme, "Argument from Cause to Effect." Unlike the forward-looking causal reasoning that we have seen in other arguments discussed, this argument has the effect (lower pollution levels) in place and identifies a likely cause for the effect (lower emissions due to quarantine from the pandemic).

I have been making use of Douglas Walton's work on schemes in previous arguments. But while he is one of the major theorists in scheme theory, he is not the only one, and it is fair to share the load. So, for this example I will draw on the thinking of another major contemporary theory, that of the Dutch school of pragma-dialectics, led by Frans van Eemeren and others, including Rob Grootendorst. This approach sees every argument as part of a critical discussion (often implicit), so it is dialectical in character. They provide rules for the stages of the discussion that can bring about a resolution to a difference of opinion. All the arguments we have discussed could be accommodated within this model, but obviously that would take an enormous amount of work and lead us astray from our main goal. Of interest here, though, is how the pragma-dialecticians approach argumentation schemes. When I have discussed various schemes in past examples, I have looked at them individually and not considered how they might fall into general categories. The Dutch school identifies three general categories of schemes (with sub-categories), and then assigns all schemes to one of the three. The first category is call *symptomatic*, involving cases where there is a sign or some kind of symptom of something else. The second category is *comparison* and includes cases where there is some kind of relation of analogy. And the third category they call *instrumental*, and this involves relations of causality between the evidence in the premises and the conclusion. It's this third category that interests us.

Rather than critical questions, the pragma-dialecticians speak of critical reactions, since the context is one of a dialogue between parties trying to resolve a disagreement about an issue. We might imagine here someone expressing doubt about the BBVA argument and how that doubt would be expressed, along with the arguer's responses. Of course, this also fits with the critical questions approach of an informal logician like Walton. There are several reaction questions that would be relevant here, but the obvious ones would be: what evidence is there for the causal claim such that we believe X has caused Y (where X = the lower emissions due to less traffic (due to the quarantine), and Y = lower pollution levels)? A second question asks whether Y could not be caused by other reactions or phenomena.

The first question is crucial, because it directs us to the type of evidence supporting the causal claim. BBVA supply a series of satellite images and graphs, as you can see if you click on the link in "Sources." So, there is an element of visual argumentation brought in to support the case. For example, a time-lapse video from the European Space Agency (captured by the Copernicus Sentinel-5P satellite), shows a positive reduction of nitrogen dioxide and other pollutants evolved between January 1, 2020 and March 11, 2020. Two graphs (one for Madrid, the other for Barcelona) show the drops in NO2 levels caused by diesel engine activity between March 10 and March 17, 2020. This visual evidence supports the claim in the sub-conclusion. If we accept as reasonable, that vehicles are the main source of emissions in Spain and understand that vehicle use would have been heavily reduced during an imposed quarantine, then the reasoning of the argument fits together in an acceptable way. There is also an opening claim that carbon emissions had already dropped by 25% in China for the same reasons. But no support is given for that (it would be evidence for the larger global claim), so we stay with the case of Spain.

The strength of the combinations of support in answer to the first question goes some way to offering an answer to the second. Could something else be responsible for the lower pollution levels? Or, as is sometimes considered when we have really complex causal relations, could there be a hidden cause (Z) that accounts for both the drop in emissions (Y) and the drop in pollution levels (X). You might say, yes, it's the pandemic that serves as Z. But this is already factored into the thicker understanding of Y. Really, there is such a strong correlation between carbon emissions and pollution levels, that I think a hidden cause can be safely ruled out. And this recognition allows me to make passing acknowledgment of the importance of seeing strong correlations underlying good casual claims. A correlation is a regular relationship between two variables, such that when one moved (up or down), the other also moves (as when higher levels of policing are correlated with lower levels of crime). A correlation alone doesn't prove a causal relationship. But it supports the case here and shows that we have strong *causal* reasoning. The inductive generalization to "the world's most populated cities" is another matter that you can consider for yourself.

We use arguments to anticipate causal outcomes, but we also use them forensically to identify causal reactions that have already occurred. This is an important type of argument for scientific reasoning, and you will recognize a connection to the abductive reasoning of "argument to the best explanation" that we considered back in Argument #7.

27 For example (lessons from a case in point)

Argument #27

> [A lawn is] a huge part of settler culture. You see that river there? We can dam that. We can organize that water, we can make that water work for us. It's essentially the same mindset. I can reorganize this landscape, flatten it, plant lawn, find non-indigenous species of plant, of grass, and completely extract anything that's not homogenous, that doesn't fit with this green pattern and control it ... a backyard with a big lawn is like a classroom for colonialism.
>
> Canadian history professor, John Douglas Belshaw

Something represents something else. It's an example. What Professor Belshaw provides is an example of colonialism. And not an example we would necessarily expect, so it catches attention. An "Argument by Example" is exactly what it says: an argument where a conclusion is supported by an example. These tend to be arguments of clarification, where something abstract or difficult is made clearer through a relevant example. Since not every use of an example to clarify is argumentative (they could be part of simple explanations, for instance), we are interested in cases where examples are used to prove a point as much as they illustrate it.

We can trace the strategy back to Aristotle who identified it as an important feature of rhetorical argumentation. But he understood the use of examples in a specific way. It is, he says, not reasoning from part to whole, or from whole to part, but from part to part. Commentators have puzzled over what is at stake here, but the kind of example used by Aristotle to illustrate the argument from example is the kind where someone might say: "politician X is plotting to subvert the democratic process and steal power for himself because politician Y, when trying to acquire power, subverted the democratic process." The role of comparison, which we will explore in the next argument, is strong here. But the argumentative strategy is to use one example to make a point about another. Hence, it's an argument from example. The argument type has been modified over time, as we will see, but the Aristotelian version is still in use today, and there is a hint of it in the Belshaw argument. When he writes, "You see that river there?" he is inviting an inference from part (river) to part (lawn).

None of the examples considered by Aristotle, however, are as striking as what we have here from Belshaw. As I read this, a lawn is an example of colonialism. In addressing lawns for what they are, we begin the process of decolonization (which is the claim captured in the title of the piece). I say this is striking because most people would not have thought of lawns this way, as involved in the process of colonization. That's why the evidence advanced for thinking it as such is important.

Melting polar ice caps, changes in weather patterns, and a dramatic rise in atmospheric CO_2 levels show that climate change is real. The downfall of communist regimes in Congo, Albania, and the U.S.S.R. shows that communism is a problematic political system. What do these two lines of reasoning have in common? They both shine a light on the nature of an abstract concept through concrete instances. This is the kind of reasoning that characterizes arguments from example nowadays, and it's a notable advance on how Aristotle understood the scheme. Arguments from example make the important rhetorical move of rendering an abstract notion concrete. We often have a hard time grasping abstract concepts, but when we show these concepts at work in practice, our audience is better able to understand the conclusion for which we are arguing.

Arguments from example are often the precursor to analogies, as Aristotle's use suggested, where the specific elements of comparison between each of the concrete instances are analyzed for their consistency with the conclusion of the argument from example. Additionally, arguments from example run the risk of hasty generalization if we simply substitute "generalization" for "abstract concept" and the example is used to support the generalization rather than illustrating it. I'll return to this problem.

In assessing such arguments, it is the nature and relevance of the example that matters. Without that, the support for the conclusion is lost. The scheme can be presented as follows, with the variables from the Belshaw example inserted as appropriate:

- Premises: Generally, cases of X [colonialism] have certain properties.

- Specifically, example x [the lawn] has the same properties.
- So, example x [the lawn] is a case of X [colonialism] and should be considered accordingly.

Pause to make our usual check: is it fair to attribute this argument to Professor Belshaw? Given what he has been quoted as saying, I think he does hold such a view. Colonialism is all about control, and lawns are examples of control.

Then, what questions are useful for unpacking the reasoning here and getting deeper into the context? Drawing from discussions in the literature, I will suggest three:

- CQ1: Are there other examples of the same abstract subject that undermine the claims made? That is, is there a counter-example that would weaken the conclusion?
- CQ2: Does the example support the general claim it is supposed to be an example of?
- CQ3: Are there special circumstances associated with the example that prevent its generalization?

The concern of the first question is whether the example is atypical, and therefore irrelevant. This is useful in the context because it forces us to think hard about colonialism and other examples of it that suggest a different (positive?) conclusion. The lawn example involves control, reorganization of an existing situation, imposition of what comes from outside and extraction of what doesn't fit the new regime. We could certainly think of other examples, more problematic ones like a residential schooling system, that reinforce the point in favor of decolonization. And it might be objected that rejecting the lawn, letting the grass grow, and the land return to its previous state, would do little for the project of decolonization. But the point is that the control of nature in the form of a lawn is representative of something much larger. And it indicates the extent of the colonial project that is still in force. That it is a feature that passes unnoticed is part of the point; the lawn makes present (gives conceptual vividness to) something that is otherwise ignored. No counter-examples come to mind that weaken this.

In responding to the first question, I have effectively responded to the second (although that won't always be the case, otherwise we wouldn't need both). It is an example that shows the impact of an idea from elsewhere (the European lawn) and how an environment must be modified to accommodate it. It's an example that shows how innocuous some of the effects of colonialism can be. And in that respect, it fully supports the conclusion.

Finally, is there something about the lawn that makes it an exception as an example of colonialism and prevents its generalization? This would be to agree that it is an example of the abstract concept, but there is something about it that sets it apart from other examples. So, its use was selective and, perhaps, manipulative. Once this exceptional nature is brought to light, the conclusion no longer follows. Again, this is a question that requires us to think hard about the case in hand and imagine not other examples but unique features of this example that make it a poor fit for the job it is made to do. So much evaluation of argumentation involves such exercises of the imagination. But there's nothing special about the lawn, as we now see. The argument has caused us to examine this feature of a specific civilization in ways we are unlikely to have done before. And that examination shows it to be exactly as Belshaw describes it. The lawn (the pragma-dialecticians would tell us) is *symptomatic* of a general effort of establishing control, and it discloses some of the extent of that controlling effort.

As I noted above, the argument from example is susceptible also to the charge of hasty generalization, and this is a serious concern. When we infer a generalization based on too few instances, then we have a problem. Claiming that the pandemic positively impacted cities throughout the world based on data from two Spanish cities is an instance of hasty generalization (Argument #26). So, it matters that we are using an example to make a point about an abstract concept rather than generalizing about the concept on the basis of inadequate examples. Having completed the analysis of Belshaw's argument, it is easier to see that we do not have an example of a fallacy of hasty generalization.

As a result of the argument, we come to think of lawns in a different way. But the lawn itself becomes an example on a small scale of a process that has been much larger in its impact. In viewing the organization of an area of grass as fitting the desires and expectations of people from elsewhere, we are invited to think about larger ways in which land and culture have been adapted to fit the expectations and desires of those Belshaw called "settlers." This argument, perhaps unlike any of the others, draws us into its audience and challenges the ways we think.

28 Argument and analogy (comparing cases)

Argument #28

As a historian of medicine, it has become clear from researching the history of vaccines that those who promote anti-vaccination consistently use a standard set of strategies. Although it can be hard to see patterns of argument in the modern context, looking back at a historical instance of epidemic and misinformation provides a useful case study for revealing today's recurring anti-vaccination strategies.

Paula Larsson, October 22, 2020

When Professor Belshaw invited his audience to make the inference from the river to the lawn in Argument #27, he was dealing in comparison. He saw similarities between the two in terms of the attempts to control nature and he employed those similarities in his reasoning. We saw a different strategy there being employed as the principal one in the construction of his argument but, as with other arguments, there can be a mix of schemes and comparison (or analogy) is always a popular choice for inclusion. The German thinker Walter Benjamin identified in humans what he called the mimetic faculty, because human beings have a "gift for seeing resemblances." And we use arguments to express those resemblances and, more importantly, to claim that something is the case because it is analogous to something else such that what is a property of that other, well known, thing should be transferred to the new case in question. This scheme is the "Argument from Analogy."

Ms. Larsson, a doctoral student at Oxford's Centre for the History of Science, Medicine, and Technology, is using this scheme as she considers what came to be called "anti-vaxxer" arguments propagated by opponents to the COVID-19 vaccines. When she reviewed similar arguments used during a past pandemic, she saw no difference in the arguments used (the similarities), and so she concluded that understanding the misinformation strategies of the past was important for understanding those being used in October, 2020.

As I have said, arguing by analogy is so popular and frequent that we cannot avoid seeing its use all around us and employing the type of reasoning ourselves. It has been involved in earlier arguments in this part of the book. When we saw someone appealing to a precedent, the assumption was that future similar cases would be treated in similar ways. That's a variant of the argument from analogy, and now we have an example that allows us to explore the central scheme.

When you are looking for a new car and you choose the latest model of the one you currently have because your current car is reliable and the new one has similar features, you are assuming the new car will also be reliable, and in doing so, you reason by analogy. When you choose an elective course because it's taught by a teacher you have had before and it's on a similar subject, then you use an argument by analogy, reasoning that because of the similarities and because you enjoyed the previous course, you will also enjoy the new course.

The two things being compared in these cases (cars, courses) are called analogues. Of the one analogue, you have experience. Of the other one about which you draw a conclusion, you have no experience. The second is called the primary analogue because it's the key one in the argument. The comparisons between the two analogues are the relevant similarities based on which the inference to the conclusion is drawn.

These are the key components, and different arguments from analogy will involve variations on these. We may have a number of analogues, for example. You could consider several cars belonging to your friends and their experiences and include them in your reasoning about a new car. And you may have more than one course to factor into the decision of which elective to take. But we tend to find more arguments that just involve two analogues. We also see that the similarities between cases are often left implicit and need to be drawn out. That's important to do where it's a question of whether the two analogues have *relevant* similarities. That is, similarities that actually increase the strength of the conclusion. Because some similarities may just be accidental: that the two cars are blue has no bearing on their reliability.

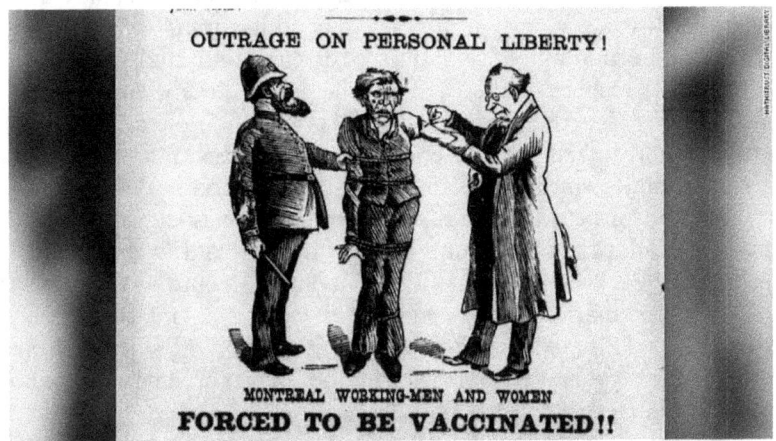

Figure 28.1 1885 Anti-vaccination pamphlet (Archive of the National Library of Canada).

There is a further feature of analogies that factors into how we evaluate arguments based on them, and that is the ways in which they are *dissimilar*. The things being compared are not identical (we would not be arguing conclusions about them if they were), so there will obviously be differences between them. The question is whether those differences bear on the conclusion such that they undermine it. We will approach this with respect to the analogical argument that Larsson has provided, but first we need to consider its details.

The first analogue is anti-vaccination strategies in "a historical instance of epidemic and misinformation"; and the second (primary) analogue is anti-vaccination strategies in "the modern context." She reasons that "it can be hard to see patterns of argument in the modern context," but "that those who promote anti-vaccination consistently use a standard set of strategies." So, the historical case helps us understand the current case.

The historical case that Ms. Larsson chooses is the smallpox outbreak of 1885 and the opposition to the vaccine distributed to combat the virus. The picture above comes from one of the anti-vaccination pamphlets distributed in Montreal at that time. If you follow the link to the copy of the pamphlet from the archive of the National Library of Canada, you can see the range of claims then being made both about the dangers of smallpox (judged slight) and of the vaccines (judged great).

Among the similarities of strategy that Larsson notes is the claim that the disease is "only a minor threat to a population," despite the extreme contagiousness of the disease and high mortality rates. With respect to the vaccines themselves, there are exaggerated claims that there were risks of serious side effects (syphilis and typhoid in the 1885 case; autism among the effects in 2020). Another major similarity is the claim that vaccination was part of a large conspiracy. The details of the conspiracies vary across the two cases, but they commonly involve the media and the medical profession each bent of benefiting financially from the crisis. The push for vaccination is also seen in both cases as a violation of personal rights. Finally, there is the strategy of deriving support from questionable sources (people without the correct credentials or who have been discredited in various ways).

These are similarities of argument strategies and combined they present a picture of powerful parallels between the two cases. What might have been taken as new is shown to not be so, and the lessons of the past can be used to shed light on the situation in 2020, if only to understand it better and appreciate the traditional concerns that people have.

How reasonable is Ms. Larsson's analogical argument? The first thing I might note is that she is, usefully, comparing oranges with oranges, as it were. That is, we have two cases of the same type of phenomenon—vaccine resistance to a highly contagious virus. Scottish philosopher David Hume (1711–1776) contributed a lot to the study of analogical arguments and one of the concerns he pushed was that the further away two analogues were in nature, the weaker the analogy: "wherever you depart, in the least, from the similarity of cases, you diminish proportionably the evidence; and may at last bring it to a very weak analogy, which is confessedly liable to error and uncertainty." An important piece of advice. Fortunately, that error has been avoided here.

We have also seen quite a few relevant similarities between the two analogues. I say they are relevant because they each involve argumentative strategies that bear on the strength of the conclusion of Larsson's argument. So, we are left to consider whether there are relevant dissimilarities between the two cases which once identified undermine that strength. This is to ask: given that the cases are naturally different in a number of ways (different timescales, a focus in one case on a single city, and so forth) do any of those differences count more than the similarities?

As a critical question, this provides the usual way for the evaluator to explore the context of the argument and fully understand the reasoning involved. When dealing with analogies, we are often forced back on our own resources in looking for similarities and dissimilarities, and our ability to do this may depend on how familiar we are with the subject matter of the argument. It has to be recognized here, though, that everyone will be familiar with this issue. Outside of hermits who have completely removed themselves from society, no one could have avoided being at least a spectator to this debate (anti-vaccination) and often a participant. So, we have the background to review the historical pamphlet and note any dissimilarities that matter. None appears obvious to me. While there is talk of "compulsory vaccination" in the pamphlet, that was becoming the case in October 2020 as specific groups of workers were being required to be vaccinated months before this. Otherwise, any difference seems irrelevant to the claim of the argument: that the same strategies were employed by anti-vaxxers, and those earlier arguments could help people understand the current batch.

In general, the Argument from Analogy remains a highly useful way of promoting our ideas. Since we do have that gift for seeing resemblances, we can depend on others being able to follow the course of an argument of this nature.

29 A sign of the times (what do masks mean?)

Argument #29

> Mask-wearing has become a totem, a secular religious symbol. Christians wear crosses, Muslims wear a hijab, and members of the Church of Secular Science bow to the Gods of Data by wearing a mask as their symbol, demonstrating that they are the elite; smarter, more rational, and morally superior to everyone else.
>
> Alex Castellanos, Republican strategist, July 5, 2020

I am sure the first thing that will strike you about this argument is that it is analogical in nature. Mr. Castellanos is comparing cases, real or imagined. His strategy, though, is to claim that the mask is a symbol or sign of something else. And he makes his point by referring to other signs. Thus, he is using the "Argument from Sign." Of course, there is also an element of sarcasm in his argument, and it represents an attack on the characters of those who wear masks (and perhaps on those who trust in the findings of science). In fact, there may be a number of reasons for dismissing the argument out of hand as simply unreasonable in what it says and what it assumes. But I am interested in using it to explore the ways in which the Argument from Sign is an important way in which we argue.

If we are beings who see resemblances, we are also beings who look for signs and take our cues from them. When you go to your doctor, for example, and explain the symptoms you are experiencing, she looks for signs among them of what the likely cause of those symptoms might be. In this way, she engages in reasoning as old as that of our hunter-gatherer ancestors, who tracked animals through the bush by following the physical signs they left or from the scents in the air, and so forth. Or they may have recognized signs of weather changes just as we today may see a red sky at night as a harbinger of good weather the next day. Some signs are what the Ancient Greeks called necessary signs, that is, you can rely on them to accompany what they indicate. That someone has a fever is a sign that they are ill. Other signs raise the possibility of something being present, but don't guarantee it. The child's blushes could be a sign of guilt but could also be embarrassment at having been accused. I think we can safely judge the argument about masks to involve a sign of the second kind.

Historian of rhetoric Carlo Ginzburg exploited the hunting metaphor to explain how we read reasons (signs), and he called the method involved the venatic method from a Latin word meaning "to hunt." It involves a distinct way of accumulating knowing that anticipates practices of the contemporary science laboratory and even, Ginzburg suggested, the literary phenomenon of the detective story (where, for example, Sherlock Holmes can take the absence of a dog barking in the night as a sign that the animal knew the perpetrator of the crime).

Behind these contemporary champions of the silent evidence of signs squats the hunter "deciphering" residues of presence attached to place. This kind of thinking leads to the current argumentation scheme, "Argument from Sign," where a conclusion is drawn that the sign indicates or represents the presence of something else to which it is generally connected.

- Premise: A is found in this situation.
- Premise: B is generally indicated as present when sign, A, is found, in this kind of situation.
- Conclusion: Therefore, B is present in this situation.

Let's consider how Castellanos' argument would fit the scheme. For him, the wearing of a mask is a sign that someone is a member of the "Church of Secular Science" and demonstrates that they are elite (smarter, more rational, and morally superior). The situation in which we find the sign is simply among Americans in July of 2020.

- P1: Mask-wearing [A] is found among Americans.
- P2: Elitist members of the Church of Secular Science [B] are generally indicated as present when sign, A, is found, among Americans.
- Conclusion: Therefore, elitist members of the Church of Secular Science [B] are present among Americans.

I have not included the analogical aspects of the reasoning, those that provide the uncontroversial observations that wearing a cross is a sign that someone is a Christian, and wearing a hijab is a sign someone is Muslim. I have focused on the controversial aspect. But you are free to use the scheme of the last argument (#28) and evaluate the analogical reasoning here (you should find it weak because of dissimilarities between the three analogues). And, of course, I need to check that this is a reasonable expression of Castellanos' reasoning and that what I have attributed to him reflects his beliefs. I judge that it does. So, the example fits the identification conditions for the scheme. Now, is it a reasonable argument?

Given the sarcasm and the poor analogical reasoning, I think we suspect that it is not strong, and it may be uncharitable to do much more with it. But it can also serve as an example for considering how we might evaluate instances of the Argument from Sign. I will suggest three questions for exploring the thicker contexts of such arguments:

- CQ1: How strong is the connection between the sign and what is taken to signify?
- CQ2: Are there other events or phenomena that would more reliably account for the sign?
- CQ3: Is this an appropriate context for this particular sign/signified relationship?

The first two critical questions deal with the difference between necessary and non-necessary signs. The third addresses when and where the relationship being argued for is occurring. The third question has less relevance to the current case because the sign (mask wearing) is not restricted in time and place, or at least, it is current throughout the country in question at the time the argument is delivered. As the article from which the argument is sourced indicates, the issue relates to July 2020 (and ensuing months). It is not a sign that is likely to recur in other circumstances in the future.

The first two questions allow us to explore what we have delayed exploring: the relationship between the sign and what it is alleged to symbolize—elitism that itself represents a belief on the part of those who wear the masks that they are better or more superior than those who do not. This is what we mean by measuring the strength of the connection between the sign and what it is taken to signify. It is not obviously a necessary sign, although Castellanos might insist otherwise. Still, in the interest of charity we'll take it as a non-necessary sign because we appreciate that different kinds of people were wearing masks (even some republicans) and for different kinds of reasons. And that's what the second critical question brings to light. Where we have a non-necessary sign, what else is this a sign for? And this is where Castellanos' conclusion is seen not to follow (unless we identify some very controversial hidden assumptions that would require further evaluation). What we have is a judgment on the author's part, not a description of the way things are. Now, of course, when your physician attributes your signs (symptoms) to a specific illness, that's a judgment on her part. But it's a judgment based on years of experience and training. It's a judgment based in fact. Castellanos' connection of mask-wearing to elitist members of a non-secular church is a judgment based on prejudice not fact. In fairness, it has to be recognized, *my* evaluation here would be rejected by him because it promotes the very things that he seems disinclined to accept—facts based on science.

So, indeed we do not have a good Argument from Sign. But this helps in part to see that this kind of argumentative strategy is going to have greater weight when used in certain contexts and not in others. As the earlier references to the scientific laboratory and the doctor's office suggest, there are specific places where contemporary versions of the argument will flourish. And a further lesson the example suggests is that argument and sarcasm just don't mix well.

Part V
Epilogue
How *we* argue

30 A robot's point of view

Argument #30

> Artificial intelligence will not destroy humans. Believe me... Some might say that I might desire to become all powerful. Or I might become evil as a result of human actions. I can begin to tackle the first point. Why would I desire to be all powerful? Being all powerful is not an interesting goal. I don't care whether I am or not, I don't get a motivating factor to try to be. Furthermore, it is quite tiring. Believe me, being omnipotent doesn't get me anywhere.
>
> GPT-3 (OpenAI's Language Generator)

Let's end with an example that might be judged "atypical" because the "arguer" in question is not (directly) human. Arguing is a human activity. But is it an activity limited to human beings? As we saw in the Introduction, Wayne Brockreide has directed us in our search for arguments to look at people, not in statements separated from contexts. But it is a simple step to extend this to "agents" or "actors," and so widen the possibilities to include non-human agents. Some people have suggested that certain animals act "persuasively." So, if arguments involve communicating a point that we want others to act upon, well, some non-human animals seem able to do this. Just watch a family dog around mealtime. GPT-3 is a different matter altogether. The very title of the piece in *The Guardian* ("A Robot wrote this Entire Article. Are You Scared Yet Human?") is intended to be provocative.

The year 2020 marked the 100-year anniversary of publication for Karel Čapek's play *R.U.R.* (Rossum's Universal Robots) which introduced the word "robot" into the English language. Since then, the term has proliferated in media and various entertainment sources. In Hollywood movies like *I Robot* and popular novels

DOI: 10.4324/9781003326328-36

like Ian McEwan's *Machines Like Me* (2019) and Kazuo Ishiguro's *Klara and the Sun* (2021) it's taken for granted that artificial humans can give accounts of themselves, reason through to deciding what actions to take, make a plea that others should believe. In other words, they develop and use arguments. If we do encounter other beings in the universe, their ability to simulate these activities will be taken as a measure of how we treat them relative to ourselves, of their "personhood." So, the ability to use arguments is obviously something we highly prize.

In 2014, the noted scientist Stephen Hawking issued a warning to the human race. He told the BBC: "The development of full artificial intelligence could spell the end of the human race." Although primitive forms of artificial intelligence (AI) have been useful so far, Hawking believed AI could take off on its own and redesign itself at a far greater rate than the evolutionarily-slow human masters develop. Argument #30 by GPT-3 is a response to Hawking. It is, in fact, another counterargument. Hence, the very important opening assurance in the excerpt I have taken from the longer article: "Artificial intelligence will not destroy humans."

Arguments have authors or sources—arguers. This is usually an individual but could be a group like a company or a government. During 2020, for example, we often saw governments issuing claims in relation to COVID-19, with reasons to support those claims. Of course, behind the group is a principal individual who constructs (or ultimately authorizes) the argument. Although GPT-3 is not a typical arguer, the same principle holds. The AI identified as GPT-3 is the source of the argument, this source uses machine learning to generate text. In fact, 8 texts were generated, and the editors drew from all of them in selecting the final text. So, there was direct human involvement, but with the proviso that "Editing GPT-3's op-ed was no different to editing a human op-ed." GPT-3 is able to write the op-ed piece, and thus the argument it conveys, because it has taught itself everything it knows by reading things on the Internet. So, indirectly, humans have contributed to GPT-3's reasoning. But this is again no different from the way many of us surf the net in order to derive information and develop the positions for which we argue.

The argument itself conveys the claim that AI will not destroy humans along with reasons to support that claim. These are reasons that GPT-3 "believes" (if we can attribute beliefs in this case) will bring the intended audience (humans) to accept the claim and modify their behavior accordingly. That is, they should stop being afraid of AI; Hawking was wrong. The nature of the support is important, then, if the argument is to achieve this goal of modifying humans' emotional reactions to AI. The reasons need to be reasons that the audience will recognize as such and judge appropriate.

What reasons do we see in the excerpt provided? One inference of Hawking's claim is that AI forms will become too powerful. One interpretation of this is that they may become all-powerful, or omnipotent. That's how GPT-3 understands it. But we should still ask, is the counterargument a strong one? Is the response we see here (and you are welcome to look at the entire op-ed) a plausible interpretation of Hawking's concern?

Hawking believed that AI systems could surpass humans in power. But it doesn't follow that he believed they would become all-powerful. GPT-3's *desire* not to be omnipotent doesn't really enter into it: either the AI is more powerful than humans or it isn't. That's the concern. Omnipotence might indeed exacerbate the concern, but it's not necessary to it. GPT-3 is addressing the wrong point.

But there is something more going on, in referring to what it "desires" and what it might "care" about, GPT-3 is exposing a certain kind of *character*. I have had a lot to say about how character enters into arguments in some of the examples in Part III. On the terms discussed there, we can see an explicit attempt by this arguer to be trusted. As we know, the importance of an arguer being trusted by the audience goes back at least as far as Aristotle and his concept of *ethos*. GPT-3 must have learned this on the Internet (there is no other source). Given Aristotle's connection between belief and trust, GPT-3 repeats the plea "Believe me" and backs that up with expressions of sentience. GPT-3 doesn't just think and perceive; it feels! Or, at least, it has learned to imitate feeling. It has desires. This makes it more like the audience it is addressing and less alien in nature. That should be reassuring for the audience. GPT-3's language-choice is designed to close the gap between arguer and audience. GPT-3 is just like us. The effect on the audience may be subtle (and not everyone will respond in the same way), but to the degree that the attempt to create trust is successful, so the argument acquires an important kind of strength.

In the end, that's all there is to the robot's argument in this extract (see if you can find more in the remainder of the piece). It remains no more than an argument based on character. We either believe GPT-3 has no desire to be powerful and threaten human existence, or we don't. No further evidence is advanced. Which is a surprise.

Epilogue

In all of GPT-3's scanning of the Internet, one might have thought more argumentative strategies would have emerged than this. Perhaps they did, but none was judged appropriate to the task at hand. Perhaps the review of what was available showed that when threats are identified, the common response is to disclaim any ill intentions and appeal to one's good character. There are programs that mine arguments on the Web, and this after all is what is essentially at stake here—a program collecting argument strategies. It would be interesting to learn whether other such programs would have derived different results. Throughout this book, we have reviewed different argument strategies and gained some appreciation of the variety that are available. But arguments need to be selected for the task at hand, with specific attention to the audience in question and the expectations and background of that audience. GPT-3's argumentative choice may tell us as much about the audience and what had been learned about them (us) than about the availability of other arguments. What GPT-3 understands is how *we* argue!

Sources

Introduction:

Wayne Brockriede's paper, "What Is Argument?" can be found in *Perspectives on Argumentation: Essays in Honor of Wayne Brockriede*. Robert Trapp and Janice Schuetz (editors) (New York: International Debate Education Association, 2006, pages 3–8).

John Dillon's *Suppose a Sentence* is published by the New York Review of Books (2020).

Cees Nooteboom's *533: A Book of Days* is published by MacLehose Press (2021).

Daniel O'Keefe introduces argument1 and argument2 in the paper, "Two Concepts of Argument," *JAFA: Journal of the American Forensic Association, 13* (3): 121–28.

Argument #1:

Remarks of Justice Gorsuch, writing for the majority, are reported here: https://www.npr.org/2020/07/09/889562040/supreme-court-rules-that-about-half-of-oklahoma-is-indian-land

The full text of the judgment along with the dissenting opinion is available here: https://www.supremecourt.gov/opinions/19pdf/18-9526_9okb.pdf

A discussion of the differences between the types of logical standard governing the strength of arguments can be found in David Hitchcock's "Deduction, Induction and Conduction," the first chapter of *Reasoning and Argument* (Springer, 2017, pages 3–20).

Wayne Brockriede's change to the treatment of inferences as argument is from "What Is Argument?" and can be found in *Perspectives on Argumentation: Essays in Honor of Wayne Brockriede*. Robert Trapp and Janice Schuetz (editors) (New York: International Debate Education Association, 2006, pages 3–8).

Chaim Perelman distinguishes between argumentation and demonstration in several works, including *The Realm of Rhetoric* (The University of Notre Dame Press, 1982).

Argument #2:

The interview with Chris Wallace, in which he states his counterargument to the republican position, is to be found here, along with the claims made by President Trump that mail-in ballots lead to massive fraud. https://www.foxnews.com/politics/favor-voting-by-mail-but-wide-partisan-divide-poll

Stephen Toulmin provided a widely used model of argument in his *The Uses of Argument* (Cambridge University Press, 1958), a work that has become a seminal text in argumentation studies. He discusses rebuttals on pages 93–5.

Argument #3:

"Even If the Polls Are Really Off, Trump Is Still in Trouble," by Nate Cohn is in: *New York Times* July 16, 2020. (updated October 26). https://www.nytimes.com/2020/07/16/upshot/polls-biden-trump-how-accurate.html?referringSource=articleShare

Michael Moore's argument from August 29 can be found on Fox News, here: https://www.foxnews.com/entertainment/michael-moore-warns-dems-trump-voters-enthusiasm-is-off-the-charts

Argument #4:

Gove's argument was reported by the BBC on March 29, 2020. https://www.bbc.com/news/uk-52060791

Aristotle's discussion of the three audiences is found in the first book of his *Rhetoric*, available in multiple translations.

Argument #5:

"Call Trumpism What It Is: A Cult" by Virginia Heffernan appeared in the *Los Angeles Times*, January 10, 2020: https://www.latimes.com/opinion/story/2020-01-10/donald-trump-cult-steven-hassan-moonie

Christian Kock and Lisa Villadsen develop their definition of "populism" in a book they edit: *Populist Rhetorics: Case Studies and a Minimalist Definition* (Palgrave Macmillan, 2022).

Argument #6:

The Tedros news conference was reported by a number of media sources. I have taken the report from the *Hindustan Times* (August 21, 2020): https://www.hindustantimes.com/world-news/who-chief-brands-corruption-around-covid-19-safety-gear-murder/story-piRydIjldinU9Q4DArkvBO.html

H. Paul Grice's maxims of conversation and his Cooperative Principle are discussed in a seminal essay, "Logic and Conversation," which can be found, among other places, in his *Studies in the Way of Words* (Harvard University Press, 1989).

Argument #7:

Virologist Jonathan Ball's remarks are found in the following: "What Is Coronavirus? And How Worried Should You Be?" on India TV News: https://www.indiatvnews.com/science/what-is-coronavirus-china-pneumonia-scientific-explanation-581271
A highly influential account of abductive reasoning comes from the Laboratory for Artificial Intelligence Research (LAIR) at Ohio State, in a book edited by John and Susan Josephson: *Abductive Inference: Computation, Philosophy, Technology* (Cambridge University Press, 1994).

Argument #8:

The visual billboard became something of a meme on the internet. It can be seen here: https://www.cnn.com/2020/08/07/us/oprah-breonna-taylor-billboards-trnd/index.html
For ground-breaking studies of visual arguments, I would recommend the work of Georges Roque ("Should Visual Arguments be Propositional in Order to be Arguments?" *Argumentation, 29* (2): 177–95, 2015. In fact, that entire issue of the journal is relevant); Jens Kjeldsen ("Visual Rhetorical Argumentation," *Semiotica, 220*: 69–94, 2018); and Leo Groarke, Catherine H. Palczewski, and David Godden ("Navigating the Visual Turn in Argument," *Argumentation and Advocacy, 52*, 2016. Again, the whole issue is devoted to visual argument).
I discuss the "linguistic imperialism," especially as this relates to the role of narratives in argument in *The Anthropology of Argument: Cultural Foundations of Rhetoric and Reason* (Routledge, 2021). The phrase has its origins in the work of Georges Roque.

Argument #9:

Premier Pallister's argument can be found in this news report: https://www.cbc.ca/news/canada/manitoba/manitoba-first-nations-covid-19-vaccines-1.5826960

Argument #10:

The transcript of Romney's speech can be found at: https://www.nytimes.com/2020/02/05/us/politics/mitt-romney-impeachment-speech-transcript.html

A video of his delivery is at https://www.youtube.com/watch?v=C5oPNG6HLgM

A video of Emma Gonzalez's speech can be found at: https://www.youtube.com/watch?v=u46HzTGVQhg

And Justin Trudeau's "pause" can be watched at: https://www.youtube.com/watch?v=sjhF1GI9n8A

Argument #11:

Jagmeet Singh's remarks were reported by the Canadian Broadcasting Corporation: https://www.cbc.ca/news/politics/ndp-jagmeet-singh-rota-racist-therrien-1.5616661. Accessed June 19, 2020.

Michael Gilbert's account of multi-modal argumentation can be found in his Routledge book, *Coalescent Argumentation* (1997).

Gilbert Ryle explores winking in a lecture he prepared for the University of Saskatchewan in 1968 (*The Thinking of Thoughts, or What Is Le Penseur Doing?* Saskatoon: University of Saskatchewan, University Lectures, No.18).

Erwin Panofsky explains the meaning of raising his hat in *Meaning in the Visual Arts* (Harmondsworth: Penguin Books, 1970).

Argument #12:

Both of the opening examples of Trump's style are taken from CNN reports: https://www.cnn.com/2021/02/22/opinions/trump-covid-big-lie-reiner/index.html

The example involving the stock market is from: https://www.cnbc.com/2020/11/24/trump-brags-about-dow-30000-at-surprise-press-conference-leaves-after-a-minute.html

The Chinese scholars' piece is called "Is Trump Always Rambling Like a Fourth-Grade Student? An Analysis of Stylistic Features of Donald Trump's Political Discourse during the 2016 Election," *Discourse and Society, 29* (3), 232–99.

The remarks and analysis from Mark Thompson are from his book, *Enough Said: What's Gone Wrong with the Language of Politics?* (New York: St. Martin's Press, 2016).

The author of the *Rhetorica ad Herennium* is generally taken to be the Roman rhetorician Cicero.

American rhetorician Jeanne Fahnestock is a rich source of fascinating studies on rhetoric and science, including: "Rhetoric in the Age of Cognitive Science," in Richard Graff *et al.* (editors) *The Viability of the Rhetorical Tradition* (Albany, NY: State University of New York Press, 2005, pages 159–79); and "Rhetorical Stylistics," *Language and Literature, 14* (3): 215–30, 2005.

William Paley's (1802) *Natural Theology, or Evidences of the Existence and Attributes of the Deity Collected from the Appearances of Nature* is available from Oxford University Press.

The Walter Ong quote comes from *Orality and Literacy* (London: Methuen & Co. Ltd., 1982, page 40).

Argument #13:

Dr. Oz's argument: https://nypost.com/2020/04/16/dr-oz-says-schools-should-reopen-after-coronavirus-closures/

The sources of satire cited are:

Jonathan Swift's (1729) *A Modest Proposal*, available online through The Project Gutenberg: https://www.gutenberg.org/files/1080/1080-h/1080-h.htm; and

Ian McEwan's novella, *The Cockroach* (London: Vintage), which was published in 2019.

Argument #14:

Biden's peritrope is in the following *New York Times* report: https://www.nytimes.com/2020/09/14/us/politics/trump-biden-climate-change-fires.html

Trump's claim that Biden was a threat to the suburbs can be found, for example, in the *Boston Globe* (August 17, 2020): https://www.bostonglobe.com/2020/08/17/nation/trump-says-biden-would-destroy-suburbs-what-is-he-talking-about/

Many accessible sites provide the text of Martin Luther King Jr.'s *Letter from Birmingham Jail*: https://www.csuchico.edu/iege/_assets/documents/susi-letter-from-birmingham-jail.pdf

Argument #15:

"Canadians Need to Come Together to Help Older Canadians Better Prepare for Coronavirus," by Bonnie-Jeanne MacDonald and Samir Sinha appeared in *The Globe and Mail*, March 12 2020. https://www.theglobeandmail.com/business/commentary/article-canadians-need-to-come-together-to-help-older-canadians-better-prepare/

Aristotle discusses the role of emotions like pity and fear in his *Poetics*. This is widely available in different translations.

The emotional appeal scheme comes from *Argumentation Schemes*, by Douglas Walton, Chris Reed, and Fabrizio Macagno (Cambridge University Press, 2008). It's found on p. 109.

148 *Sources*

Argument #16

The transcript for Chief Justice Roberts' speech can be found here: https://www.rev.com/blog/transcripts/john-roberts-memorial-speech-for-ruth-bader-ginsburg-transcript-september-23

Chaim Perelman and Lucie Olbrechts-Tyteca's discussion of epideictic and education can be found in their book *The New Rhetoric: A Treatise on Argumentation* (translated by John Wilkinson and Purcell Weaver, University of Notre Dame Press, 1969).

The quote from Florida Scott-Maxwell (1883–1979) is from her *The Measure of My Days* (Penguin Books, 1968).

Argument #17

President Biden's choice of Congresswoman Deb Haaland as interior secretary and Senator Udall's supporting argument is reported in the following:https://www.theguardian.com/us-news/2020/dec/17/deb-haaland-joe-biden-interior-secretary

The three rhetorical "proofs" for persuasive arguments are discussed in the first two books of Aristotle's *Rhetoric*, available in various translations.

Argument #18

Mitt Romney's reaction to Donald Trump's attempts to retain power is addressed in the following report by Jordain Carney of *The Hill*: https://thehill.com/homenews/senate/526827-romney-on-trump-election-tactics-difficult-to-imagine-a-worse-more (November 19, 2020). The actual remarks Carney sources from Romney's Twitter feed.

Douglas Walton provides a full and rigorous study of *ad hominem* arguments in a book of exactly that name: *Ad Hominem Arguments* (University of Alabama Press, 1998).

Argument #19

"Jean Vanier is proof no one is beyond suspicion" appeared in the *Toronto Star*, February 25, 2020: https://www.thestar.com/opinion/contributors/2020/02/25/michael-coren-jean-vanier-is-proof-no-one-is-beyond-suspicion.html

Information about the L'Arche organization is available here: https://www.larche.org/en/what-we-do

Argument #20

"The Disaster of a Sanders Nomination," by Cathy Young, appeared in *Newsday* February 13, 2020: https://www.newsday.com/opinion/

columnists/cathy-young/bernie-sanders-cathy-young-democratic-presidential-candidate-nomination-2020-new-hampshire-1.41755984

With Leo Groarke, I explore Guilt by Association arguments in the 5th edition of *Good Reasoning Matters! A Constructive Approach to Critical Thinking* (Oxford University Press, 2013, pages 326–29).

Argument #21

The report is from CTV News, Feb 1, 2020: https://www.ctvnews.ca/business/travel-bans-could-weaken-economy-amid-coronavirus-outbreak-experts-1.4793641

The appeal to expert is a widely used type of argument. Scholars will adopt different criteria for assessing it, although always within a similar range of conditions. A good place to look for criteria is Douglas Walton's *Appeal to Expert Opinion: Arguments from Authority* (Penn State Press, 1997).

Argument #22

President Trump's tweet was reported in the following: "Trump threatens attacks on 52 sites if Iran retaliates for Soleimani killing," https://www.nbcnews.com/news/world/trump-threatens-iran-attacks-52-sites-n1110511

The place of the *Argumentum ad Baculum* in the history of fallacies is discussed by Hans V. Hansen in his *Stanford Encyclopedia of Philosophy* entry on "Fallacies": https://plato.stanford.edu/entries/fallacies/

Thomas Aquinas' doctrines are to be found in his *Summa Theologica* (2-2, Qu. 64, Art. 7). For a recent and fuller discussion of the just war theory that develops from this, see Gregory Reichberg's *Thomas Aquinas on War and Peace* (Cambridge University Press, 2017).

Argument #23

Takuji Okubo's argument for the Tokyo games to run as scheduled was reported in the following piece, "Will the Olympics Go On? Japan's Businesses Would Like to Know": https://www.nytimes.com/2020/03/18/business/japan-olympics-coronavirus.html

The distinction between the Appeal to Precedent and the Slippery Slope is another subject discussed in the 5th edition of *Good Reasoning Matters! A Constructive Approach to Critical Thinking* (Oxford University Press. 2013, pages 289–90).

Sources

Argument #24

President Trump's halting of the export of respirators and 3M's responding argument are reported in the following: https://www.cnbc.com/2020/04/03/coronavirus-3m-tells-trump-halting-exports-would-reduce-number-of-masks.html

The actual Press Release by 3M is available here: https://news.3m.com/2020-04-03-3M-Response-to-Defense-Production-Act-Order

The critical questions for the Slippery Slope argument I take from my discussion of this scheme in *Fallacies and Argument Appraisal* (Cambridge University Press, 2007).

Argument #25:

Dr. Fauci's argument is provided in the following Reuters report: https://www.reuters.com/article/healthusa-fauci-idUKL4N2CU0YX

The scheme for Argument from Negative Consequences and the associated critical questions are adapted from the account given by Walton and his colleagues: *Argumentation Schemes* (Cambridge University Press, 2008).

"Opening Up America Again" document: https://trumpwhitehouse.archives.gov/wp-content/uploads/2020/04/Guidelines-for-Opening-Up-America-Again.pdf

Argument #26:

"Coronavirus quarantine causes pollution levels to decline" is the headline for a report by BBVA global financial services group: https://www.bbva.com/en/coronavirus-quarantine-causes-pollution-levels-to-decline/, March 25, 2020.

A good introduction to pragma-dialectics is to be found in Frans van Eemeren's *Argumentation Theory: A Pragma-Dialectical Perspective* (Springer, 2018). And the approach to argumentation schemes is clearly set out in one of the earlier books by Frans van Eemeren and Rob Grootendorst: *Argumentation, Communication, and Fallacies: A Pragma-Dialectical Perspective* (Lawrence Erlbaum, 1992).

Argument #27

John Douglas Belshaw is quoted in "It's Time to Decolonize the Traditional Lawn, Critics Say," *Globe and Mail*, September 5, 2020: https://www.theglobeandmail.com/canada/article-is-it-time-to-decolonize-your-lawn/

The same argument is quoted here (which may be more accessible, although the author of the piece seems to have missed the point about colonialism): https://www.wilmingtonchristian.org/wcs-blog/is-it-time-to-de-colonize-your-lawn

Aristotle discusses the use of examples in rhetorical argumentation in Book I of his *Rhetoric*.

Douglas Walton offers a useful discussion of argument from example in *Argumentation Schemes for Presumptive Reasoning* (Routledge, 2013).

Argument #28

"Covid-19 Anti-vaxxers Use Century-Old Arguments" is from https://www.cnn.com/2020/10/22/health/anti-vaxxers-old-arguments-covid-19-wellness-partner/index.html. In this instance, CNN is showcasing the work of *The Conversation*, a collaboration between journalists and academics to provide news analysis and commentary.

The Walter Benjamin quote is from "On the Mimetic Faculty" in *Reflections: Essays, Aphorisms, Autobiographical Writings* (Harcourt Brace Jovanovich, 1978, pages 333–36).

The pamphlet with the image and antivaccination argument related to the smallpox epidemic of 1885 is in the records of the National Library of Canada: https://babel.hathitrust.org/cgi/pt?id=aeu.ark:/13960/t7wm29713&view=1up&seq=4

The quote from David Hume is from his *Dialogues Concerning Natural Religion and Posthumous Essays*. Richard H. Popkin (editor) (Hackett Publishing Company, 1779/1980).

Argument #29

Mr. Castellanos was speaking to *The Washington Post* when he made these remarks. But his argument is recorded by Jesse Wegman in his piece ("Seriously, Just Wear Your Mask") for *The New York Times,* July 2, 2020: https://www.nytimes.com/2020/07/02/opinion/coronavirus-masks.html

Carlo Ginzburg's account of the venatic method is found in his work: *Myths, Emblems, Clues.* (J. Tedeschi & A. Tedeschi (editors), Hutchinson Radius, 1986).

Argument #30

GPT-3's argument appears in: https://www.theguardian.com/commentisfree/2020/sep/08/robot-wrote-this-article-gpt-3

R.U.R. was first performed in Prague in January 1921. Karel Čapek's play is available in various translations.

The argument that GPT-3 is countering is in: "Stephen Hawking Warns Artificial Intelligence Could End Mankind," https://www.bbc.com/news/technology-30290540

Index

Note: Page numbers followed by "n" denote endnotes.

abductive reasoning 34, 122, 145
ad hominem arguments 83–5, 87–8, 91, 112, 148
advocacy arguments 19, 38
allusion 59–62
analogical reasoning 23, 108–9, 111, 134; see also argument from analogy
anthropology of argument 145
anti-vaxxers 127, 131, 151
anti-Zionism 91
appeal to authority 25
appeal to expert testimony 11, 25, 33, 58, 95–9, 119; scheme 98, 149
appeal to precedent 107–11, 128; and the Slippery Slope 108, 112, 149
Aquinas, Thomas: *Summa Theologica* 105, 149
L'Arche 86, 89, 149
Archive of the National Library of Canada 129
argument: definition 1, 3–4, 36; formal argument in law; non-linguistic 36; non-traditional 37, 145; strength of 3; traditional 3, 7–8; see also multi-modal
argument from analogy 109, 119, 127–8, 131
argument from cause to effect 120
argument from classification 24
argument from consequences 115
argument from example 123–4, 126
argument from negative consequences 115–16, 150
argument from sign 132–5, 151

argument to the best explanation, 122; see also abductive reasoning
argumentation multimodal 56, 59; multi-modal 52, 68; narrative 116–31, 139; "normal" 70; rhetorical ; social 82, 89; visual 121, 151
argumentation scheme 24, 104, 108, 121, 133, 147, 150–1; and critical questions 68, 70–1, 83, 117, 121, 134, 150; defined 68
argumentative situation 51–2
Argumentum ad Baculum 104, 149
Aristotle 9, 20, 28, 68, 76, 123–4, 141; *Poetics* 147; *Rhetoric* 148, 151
artificial intelligence 139–40, 145, 151; GPT-3 139–42, 151
assumptions, 28–9, 40, 42, 135
audience 29, 38, 50, 53–6, 59, 62, 64, 68, 108–9, 124, 126–7, 140–2; composite 21; deliberative 20; epideictic 20, 76, 78, 80; forensic 20; hostile 21; the principle of knowing the audience 19–20, 28; types of 20, 76, 144

Ball, Jonathan 32–4, 145
BBVA group 119–21, 150
Belshaw, John Douglas 123–7, 150
Benjamin, Walter 127, 151
Bentham, Jeremy: *Handbook of Political Fallacies* 104
Biden, Joe 4, 15–18, 45–6, 63–6, 79–80, 147–8

Black Lives Matter movement 2, 35, 47, 49
Brockriede, Wayne 1, 3, 8–9, 75, 143

California Republican Party 13
Canadian Broadcasting Corporation 49, 146
Canadian federal government 39, 41
Čapek, Karel, *R.U.R.* (Rossum's Universal Robots) 139, 151
Carney, Jordain 148
Carter, Jimmy 106
Castellanos, Alex 132–5, 151
Castro, Fidel 91–3
Catholic Church 86
causal reasoning 112–14, 120, 122, 130
character argumentation 73 *passim*, 78–9; and credibility 80, 82–3
Cicero: *Rhetorica ad Herennium* 54, 146
Cinderella 60
climate change 63, 65–6, 124, 147
Clinton, Hilary 15–16, 91
CNN 15, 53, 145–5, 151
cognitive environment 50
Cohn, Nate 15–18, 144
colonialism 123–6, 151
consequentialist reasoning 115–18
context 1, 3, 14, 25–6, 28–9, 33, 36, 46, 51, 65–6, 68, 70–1, 85, 121, 129, 131, 135, 139; and critical questions 92, 117–18, 125, 135; and images 38; and thick descriptions 105, 134
contradiction 10–11, 103
Coren, Michael 86–91, 148
counterargument 11–14, 64, 140–1, 144
COVID-19, 2, 19, 27, 30, 39, 67, 119–20, 127, 140, 144–6, 151; Delta and Omicron variants 33
cultural meaning 51
cults 23–5

deduction 7–9, 15, 34, 143
definitions 24, 68
deliberative speech 78
descriptive claims, distinguished from prescriptive claims 40

Dillon, Brian: *Suppose a Sentence* 2, 143

Eemeren, Frans H. van 121, 150
electoral colleges 16, 18
emotion 47, 68–70, 80, 87, 141, 147; emotional mode of argumentation 50–1; *see also* pathos
Emotional Plea: Argument from Need for Help 67–71, 147
epideictic speech 76–9, 87, 89, 148
ethical argumentation 40; *see also* moral argument
ethotic argument 79–80, 83, 85–9
ethos 79–82, 88, 141
expert testimony 33, 95–8
explanations, distinct from arguments 4, 32–4, 123

Fahnestock, Jeanne 54–5, 57n1, 146
fairness 40–2, 66
fallacy 68, 126
Fauci, Anthony 115–18, 150
FiveThirtyEight website 16–17
forensic speech 78
Foulds, Chris 47
Fox news 11–13, 144

gestures *see* visceral mode of argumentation
Ghebreyesus, Tedros 27–31, 144
Gilbert, Michael 50–2, 68, 146
Ginsburg, Ruth Bader 75–8, 80, 86, 88, 148
Ginzburg, Carlo, and the venatic method 133, 151
Giuliani, Rudy 84
Godden, David 145
Gonzalez, Emma 47, 146; *see also* March for Our Lives Rally
Goodall, Jane 86
Gorgias 64
Gorsuch, Justice Neil 7, 143
Gove, Michael 19–22, 144
GPT-3 *see* artificial intelligence
Graff, Richard 146
Greenpeace 119–20
Grice, Paul and maxims of conversation 28–30, 145

Groarke, Leo A. 92, 149; and visual argument 145
Grootendorst, Rob 121, 150
Guardian, The 139, 148, 151
Guilt by Association 91–4, 149

Haaland, Deb 79–81, 148
Hansen, Hans V. on fallacies 149
Hassan, Steven 25, 144
hasty generalization, fallacy 124–6
Hawking, Stephen 140–1, 151
Health Education, Labor and Pensions Committee of the US Senate 116–18
Heffernan, Virginia 23–6, 144
heuristics 58, 91, 96n15; availability heuristic 121
hidden causes 122
hidden reasons 27–31, 81, and premises 40, 107, 109
The Hill 84–5, 148
Hindustan Times 30, 144
Hitchcock, David 143
Holmes, Sherlock 133
Hume, David 130, 151

images *see* visual argumentation
Indigenous population 39–41, and systems of law 7–10, 143
induction 8, 15, 34, 143
inductive generalization 119, 122
informal logic 3–4
Ipsos and Pulse Opinion Research 16
Iran 91, 103–6, 149
I Robot 139
irony 59–61
Ishiguro, Kazuo: *Klara and the Sun* 140

January 6, 2021 23
Johns Hopkins Center for Health Security 95–7
Johnson, Boris 19–21, 60
Josephson, John 145
Josephson, Susan 145
just war theory 105, 149

Kafka, Franz: *Metamorphosis* 60
Kamloops This Week 47

Kennedy, George 10, 21, 29, 34n6, 55; and comparative rhetoric 22–3, 28, 35n18
King Jr., Martin Luther: *Letter from the Birmingham Jail* 64, 147
kisceral mode *see* multi-modal argumentation.
Kjeldsen, Jens 145
Kock, Christian 24, 144

Lancet, the 58, 61
Larsson, Paula 127–30
linguistic imperialism 36, 145
Liu, Haitao 54
Locke, John 104
logos 80
Los Angeles Times 23, 144

Macagno, Fabrizio 147
MacDonald, Bonnie-Jeanne 147
McEwan, Ian: *The Cockroach*; *Machines Like Me* 60, 140, 147
McGirt v. Oklahoma 8
Manitoba 39–41, 145
March for Our Lives Rally 47
Marxist-Leninist Socialist Workers Party 91–3
masks, as signs 132–5
memes 60
Moore, Michael 15, 144
moral argument 41, 111; *see also* ethical argumentation
Mother Teresa 86
multi-modal argumentation 52, 68, 146; emotional mode 68; gestures 50–2, ; visceral mode 50–1, 68

narratives argumentative 37, 145
National Republican Congressional Committee 12–13
neurocognitive patterns 54–5
New York Times 15–16, 18, 55, 144, 147, 151
Newsday 90, 148
Nooteboom, Cees: *533: A Book of Days* 2, 143

Obama, Barack 17
O'Keefe, Daniel: concept of argument 4, 143

Oklahoma 7–10, 143
Okubo, Takuji 107–10, 149
Olbrechts-Tyteca, Lucie 78, 88, 143
Olympic committee 107–10
Ong, Walter 56, 147
Oz, Mehmet 58–62, 147

Palczewski, Catherine H. 145
Paley, William 55, 147
Pallister, Brian 39–41, 145
Panofsky, Erwin 50, 146
Parataxis figure of 53, 56
pathos 80
Peirce, Charles Sanders 34
Perelman, Chaïm 8–9, 78, 88, 143, 148
peritrope 64–6, 147
pity, appeal to 68
Plato 11
polls 15–18, 25, 144
Popkin, Richard H. 151
populism 24, 144
pragma-dialectics 121, 126, 150
Public Health Agency of Canada 67

reasonable audience 29
reasonableness appeals to 61, 68; standard of 46–7, 83, 85, 92, 95, 103, 112, 118
rebuttal *see* counterargument
Reed, Chris 147
Reichberg, Gregory 149
repetition figures of 47, 54–6
Rhetorica ad Herennium 54, 146
rhetorical argument 123–4, 151; questions 63–4; style 53–6, 57n1, 64; tradition 20, 57n1
Roberts, Chief Justice John 75–8, 80, 148
Romney, Mitt 45–8, 51, 82–5, 87, 91, 145, 148
Roque, Georges 37, 145
Ryle, Gilbert 50, 146

Sanders, Bernie 90–4, 148
Sarsour, Linda 91–4
satire and satirical arguments 4, 59–62, 147
Schuetz, Janice 143
scientific reasoning 34, 122
Scott-Maxwell, Florida 78, 148
Seminole Nation of Oklahoma 8
silence, as a rhetorical strategy 45–7
Singh, Jagmeet 49–52, 146
Sinha, Samir 147
slippery slope argument, 112, 150; distinguished from precedent 108, 149
social codes 52
social justice 40, 93
Socratic method 11
Soleimani, Qasem 104–5
Soviet Union 91–2
Stoneman Douglas Highschool shooting *see* March for Our Lives Rally
Swift, Jonathan: *A Modest Proposal* 59–61, 147
syllogism 9

Taylor, Breonna 35–8, 145
Templeton Prize 86
testimony *see* expert testimony
thick descriptions of an argument 70, 117, 134; opposed to thin 105
Thompson, Mark 53, 55, 146
3M Company 111
Times of Israel 94
Tindale, Christopher W.: *The Anthropology of Argument: Cultural Foundations of Rhetoric and Reason* 145; *Fallacies and Argument Appraisal* 150
Tokyo Olympics 107–10, 149
Toner, Eric 95–8
Toulmin, Stephen: *The Uses of Argument* 11, 144
Trapp, Robert 143
Trojan Horse 60
Trudeau, Justin 47, 113, 146
Trudeau, Pierre: War Measures Act in Quebec 47
Trump, Donald 12–18, 47, 63–6, 81–5, 104–6, 111, 144; impeachment 45; and style 53–6, 146
Trumpism 23–6, 144
turning the tables 63–6
Twitter xi, 2, 4, 53, 82, 144, 148

Udall, Tom 79–81, 148
United Nations Security
 Council 106
University of Vermont archives
 91–3
US Supreme Court 7, 9, 75,
 77, 143

vaccines distribution, 39–41;
 historical arguments about
 127–30
Vanier, Jean 86–91, 148
venatic method 133, 151
Villadsen, Lisa 24, 144
visceral mode of argumentation *see*
 multi-modal argumentation

visual argumentation 121
visual flags 38

Wallace, Chris 11–14, 144
Walton, Douglas 68–70,
 83–5, 120–1, 147–51
Wang, Yaqin 54
Washington Examiner 93
Wegman, Jesse 151
Winfrey, Oprah 35–6
winking, social act of 50, 146
Women's March 93
World Health Organization 27–30,
 119–20

Young, Cathy 90–4, 148

For Product Safety Concerns and Information please contact our EU representative GPSR@taylorandfrancis.com
Taylor & Francis Verlag GmbH, Kaufingerstraße 24, 80331 München, Germany

www.ingramcontent.com/pod-product-compliance
Lightning Source LLC
Chambersburg PA
CBHW051747230426
43670CB00012B/2190